A PASSION
FO
PO

D0827307

A PASSION
FOR THE
POSSIBLE

A Message to U.S. Churches

Westminster/John Knox Press
Louisville, Kentucky

Scripture quotations from the New Revised Standard Version of the Bible are copyright © 1989 by the Division of Christian Education of the National Council of the Churches of Christ in the U.S.A., and are used by permission.

Excerpt from "All Along the Watchtower" by Bob Dylan. Copyright © 1968 by Dwarf Music. All rights reserved. International copyright secured. Reprinted by permission.

Book design by Drew Stevens

Cover photo by Jann Cather Weaver

First edition

Published by Westminster/John Knox Press
Louisville, Kentucky

This book is printed on acid-free paper that meets the American National Standards Institute Z39.48 standard. ∞

PRINTED IN THE UNITED STATES OF AMERICA
9 8 7 6 5 4

Library of Congress Cataloging-in-Publication Data

Coffin, William Sloane.
    A passion for the possible : a message to U.S. churches / William Sloane Coffin. — 1st ed.
        p.   cm.
    ISBN 0–664–25428–4 (alk. paper)

    1. Church and social problems—United States.   I. Title.
HN39.U6C56   1993
261.8'3'0973—dc20
                                                    93–8022

FOR
JESSICA
AND
WIL

"Let us not talk falsely now,
The hour is getting late."
Bob Dylan

CONTENTS

INTRODUCTION

THE MOMENT IS RIPE. And William Blake properly warned:

> If you trap the moment before it is ripe
> The tears of repentance you'll certainly wipe.
> But if once you let the ripe moment go
> You'll never wipe off the tears of woe.

Having won itself a new chance in the November elections of 1992, America may well be facing a future far
preferable to the one we could have predicted only a
short while ago. Certainly a better world is both imagin-
able and feasible. But, as always, if there's a way to the
better, it lies in first taking a full look at the worst.

To a degree almost inconceivable, we Americans have
neglected the plight of the poor, the bloat of the military,
the size of the deficit, the sorrow of the aged and infirm.
An estimated 135,000 guns attend school every day; our
children are murdering one another. The United States is
today spiritually devastated, the most crime-ridden, drug-
ridden, debt-ridden nation on the face of the earth.

Not that other countries are sinless, far from it. As Yeats
declared: "There is not left a virtuous nation, and the best
of us walk by candlelight." We talk of a fragile planet, but

1

it's really the human race that is fragile, and it is far from certain that we care enough for posterity to pay the price of its survival.

It is that concern for our children and their children which prompts this message to the churches of America. I believe they could play a significant role in saving the planet. And I say that with no illusions. Most church boats don't like to be rocked. They would rather lie at anchor than go places on stormy seas. But over a lifetime I've seen many hoist sail and leave harbor, just as I've seen genuine saints on Sunday morning.

Although this message is addressed primarily to those whose loyalties and language I share, if non-Christians and nonbelievers find merit in it, I shall be gratified, for only together can we secure the safer, saner future our children at this moment seem unlikely to inherit.

As I see it, the primary religious task these days is to try to think straight. Seeing clearly is more important even than good behavior, for redemptive action is born of vision. Religious faith, far from being a substitute for thought, makes better thinking possible. You can't think straight with a heart full of fear, for fear seeks safety, not truth. If your heart's a stone, you can't have decent thoughts—either about personal relations or about international ones. A heart full of love, on the other hand, has a limbering effect on the mind. And Christians should never think they honor the greater truth they find in Christ by ignoring truths found elsewhere.

The issues I have chosen to discuss are among those which seem crucial to the nation's well-being and to the planet's survival. All are controversial and, for the most part, intensely political. But let no one say that for being more political an issue is less spiritual. A fine prayer reads: "To those who have hunger, give bread; to those who have bread, give a hunger for justice." That over 20 million

Americans cannot read the poison warnings on a can
under the sink, a letter from their children's teacher, or the
front page of a newspaper—such a failure in the richest
nation in the world is more spiritual than political.

The chapters that follow are purposely short, intended
to provoke discussion, not to exhaust the subject matter. I
am well aware that there is always greater consensus
about what is wrong than about how to right the wrong.
But if, without defensiveness, people can face and discuss
rather than avoid or deny controversial issues, good results
are all but inevitable.

There are plenty of reasons to be pessimistic about our
immediate future. How can you be optimistic when the
maximum that is politically feasible still falls short of the
minimum necessary to be truly effective, whether the issue
be the deepening poverty in America, the national debt increasing at $13,000 a second, or the survival of the planet's
environment? But the political climate can and may well
change. And in the meantime, if not optimistic, we can be
hopeful, hope being a state of mind independent of the
state of the world. If faith puts us on the road, hope is
what keeps us there. It enables us to keep a steady eye on
remote ends. It makes us persistent when we can't be optimistic, faithful when results elude us. For like nothing
else in the world, hope arouses a passion for the possible,
a determination that our children not be asked to shoulder
burdens we let fall. Hopeful people are always critical of
the present but only because they hold such a bright view
of the future. To lay claim to this future today, American
Christians should live at loving odds with their country
and world, much as the biblical prophets and Jesus himself lived at dangerous odds with the Israel and the world
of their day.

1

A VISION OF
THE FUTURE

"Where there is no vision, the people perish."
Proverbs 29:18, KJV

"It is time we steered by the stars,
not by the lights of each passing ship."
General Omar Bradley

"Who is there big enough to love the whole planet?"
E. B. White, December 1941

"Peace is people talking together
with a heart in between them."
Bobby, age 8

OF ALL MICHELANGELO'S POWERFUL FIGURES, none is more poignant than the man in the *Last Judgment* being dragged down to hell by demons, one hand over one eye and in the other a look of dire recognition. He understood, but too late.

It's a familiar story, isn't it? Rarely do we see the truth that stares us in the face until it *hits* us in the face. A crisis is seldom a crisis until it is validated by disaster. Michelangelo was right: hell is truth seen too late.

I recall his figure because I am convinced that we too are hell-bent unless we open our eyes and see the most significant challenge of the twentieth century. It is that the world as a whole now has to be managed, and not just its parts. The only questions are how and by whom.

Until recently it was enough to be concerned with the parts. It was enough to worry that this part of the world couldn't protect itself against that part. Today it's the whole that can't protect itself against the parts.

In World War II, nations at war targeted one another. Today the whole world lives on the target of World War III. If we do not soon stop the production and proliferation of weapons of mass destruction, the whole planet may end up a dreary waste of ash and cinder, silenced by death. Likewise, if we do not soon evolve a life-style more considerate of the environment, we could all cook slowly in a stew of industrial pollutants. And if Abraham Lincoln was right, that a nation cannot long endure half slave, half free, then it is unreasonable to expect the world long to endure partly prosperous, mostly miserable.

In short, the planet is at risk, and in an order of magnitude never previously even imagined. No longer is the survival unit a single nation or single anything; it is the entire human race plus the environment. Beyond saluting their flags, children in school should pledge allegiance "to the earth, and to the flora, fauna, and human life that it supports; one planet indivisible, with clean air, soil, and water, economic justice, freedom, and peace for all."

As for Christians, it is time we stopped retreating from the giant social issues of the day into the pygmy world of private piety. The chief religious question is not, "What must I do to be saved?" but rather, "What must we all do to save God's creation?"

I believe the religious community has the saving vision. It is the ancient prophetic vision of human unity, now become an urgent, pragmatic necessity. According to this vision, we all belong one to another, every one of us five and a half billion people on this planet. That's the way God made us; from a Christian point of view, Christ died to keep us that way, which means that our sin is only and always that we put asunder what God has joined together. Human unity is not something we are called on to create, only to recognize and make manifest. Territorial discrimination has always been as evil as racial, as Pablo Casals recognized when he asked: "To love one's country is a splendid thing, but why should love stop at the border?"

Were religious people everywhere to implement the unity they profess, a unity universal and eternal, the future would appear far more promising.

But now we have to confront an irony profound and complicated. At the very moment in history when the mere notion of national sovereignty is about as obsolete as was states' rights when Jefferson Davis preached it and Robert E. Lee fought for it, the three most powerful movements in the world are nationalism, ethnicity, and racism.

All three can be attributed largely to sin: once again we are putting asunder what God has joined together.

But it would be a mistake to leave it at that and not recognize the many legitimate differences that exist within our common humanity. Nationalism, ethnicity, race, gender, our different sexual orientations—all have their rightful place, and the universalism that is their opposite tends to blur, deny, and too often repress what is particular about them. It is totally understandable that people want to preserve and deepen their roots in their own land, language, and culture, and that they also want to champion a gender or races that for so long have been so cruelly maligned. It should come as no surprise that everywhere people are asserting the particular over and against the universal. It is not even surprising that nations themselves are breaking up, for while the nation-state is clearly too small for the big problems of life, nation-states often appear too big for the small problems of life.

The challenge today is to seek a unity that celebrates diversity, to unite the particular with the universal, to recognize the need for roots while insisting that the point of roots is to put forth branches. What is intolerable is for differences to become idolatrous. When absolutized, nationalism and ethnicity, race, and gender are reactionary impulses. They become pseudoreligions, brittle and small, without the power to make people great. No human being's identity is exhausted by his or her gender, race, ethnic origin, or national loyalty. Human beings are fully human only when they find the universal in the particular, when they recognize that all people have more in common than they have in conflict, and that it is precisely when what they have in conflict seems overriding that what they have in common needs most to be affirmed. Human rights are more important than a politics of identity, and religious people should be notorious boundary crossers.

It is undeniable that present national policies and national structures are not only incapable of solving worldwide problems, but, in fact, exacerbate them. Thus the future is slipping away from us. To preserve the planet we need minimally and immediately to moderate national sovereignty and to increase global loyalty.

As Norman Cousins has reminded us, Americans have a helpful analogy in their history. After successfully declaring their independence from Great Britain, the original thirteen colonies decided to govern themselves according to the so-called Articles of Confederation. But the Articles mirrored more than they resolved the problems of the day. So, to their great credit, our spiritual forebears quickly abandoned the Articles of Confederation in favor of a constitution that demanded the sacrifice of a certain amount of independence for the sake of a stronger, more effective whole.

The United Nations today is the Articles of Confederation. The United Nations Charter is a pre-atomic document. The United Nations was organized for an era already over. It failed to heed Albert Einstein's warning: "The release of the power of the atom has changed everything except our way of thinking. Thus we drift toward a catastrophe of unparalleled magnitude."

Some time ago, a Latin American delegate at the UN observed wryly: "Around here [at the UN] things tend to disappear. If it's a conflict between two small nations and we deal with it, the conflict disappears. If it's a conflict between a small and a large nation, the small nation disappears. And if it's a conflict between two large nations, then the UN disappears."

The UN disappears because not one of the more than 180 states of the world has seen fit to surrender one iota of its sovereignty. The UN hasn't failed the world; the world has failed the UN. The nations of the world have refused to see the truth staring them in the face. All have failed to make what we might call the magnum conceptual leap forward that the times demand.

To quote Einstein again: "Imagination is more important than knowledge." It is not enough to analyze the world as it is and ask, "Why?"; we need also to imagine the world as it might be and ask, "Why not?"

We need to imagine a world whose citizens will be as mindful of international law as they are of domestic law and so obey the decisions of the World Court at The Hague.

We need to imagine a world whose peacekeeping forces will be larger than any national force. Only so can there be genuine collective security where the strength of all is for the defense of each.

We need to imagine a world whose international agencies will be supported by an international income tax, based on gross national product or perhaps energy consumption. If this seems preposterous, let us recall that so did a national income tax when, at the turn of the century, it was being urged upon Americans by William Jennings Bryan.

We cannot imagine a world free of conflict, for the horizons of the world will always be darkened by dissension. But we can imagine a world free of violent conflict, free of toxic wastes, one in which the yawning chasm that presently divides rich and poor would be greatly narrowed.

If all the above, and especially the vision of a world beyond war, seem hopelessly utopian, that may simply reflect how far we have slipped behind in a schedule we should have kept had we been serious about saving the planet.

The great issues of our time are clearly ethical. That suggests that churches and seminaries would do well to stop separating theology from ethics—which is always bad theology. How, after all, can you be holy without being ethical? Isn't justice the moral test of spirituality? Important as is the purity of dogma, it is never as significant as the integrity of love. Creeds are signposts, love is the hitching post. To deny the ultimacy of love is not a distortion of the gospel, it's desertion. It is to use the God who "made of one blood all nations of the earth" to justify the continued spilling of that blood. Religious people need to ponder less their many and differing creeds, and more how they might develop a single ethic of global responsibility.

Such an ethic would address crucial tasks, which here I shall only outline, but in subsequent chapters will seek to elaborate. As earlier implied, the planet is threatened on three major fronts: (1) by the production, modernization, and proliferation of weapons of mass destruction; (2) by the way we live in our environment as in a hotel, leaving the mess for others to clean up; and (3) by a Dickensian world of wretched excess and wretched despair. In positive terms, we should make the conquest of war, the preservation of nature, and the pursuit of social justice "our grand preoccupation and magnificent obsession" (Norman Cousins).

Above all, and at almost any risk, we must get the world beyond war. It is not enough to wish for peace, we have to will it, to pray, think, struggle for peace as if the whole world depended upon it, as indeed it does.

I am well aware that Jesus didn't tell the Roman centurion to leave the service, nor did John the Baptist tell the soldiers who came to be baptized to lay down their arms. But the scale and horror of modern warfare make it totally unacceptable as a means of settling differences between nations. Weapons in John's day compared to weapons in ours are as the lightning bug to the lightning.

Let Christians remember that only God has the authority to end life on this planet, the only thing human beings have is the power. I believe that, in the sight of God, the mere possession of nuclear weapons must be an abomination comparable to the mere possession of slaves some one hundred and fifty years ago. And the analogy can be pressed, for as in the previous century the argument was between those who wanted to humanize the institution of slavery and those who wanted to abolish it, so today a similar argument exists between those who want to limit the hideous effects of nuclear weapons and those who want to abolish them. I believe we need a new abolitionist movement.

We need first, a comprehensive test ban treaty, then quickly thereafter an agreed-on halt to the production of all nuclear, chemical, and biological weapons. The disarmament presently taking place needs to be accelerated worldwide, and to take place under some form of stringent international inspection. To see that disarmament occurs rapidly and responsibly should be a primary task assigned our Secretary of Defense. On-site inspection without right of refusal would of course constitute a significant step in moderating national sovereignty and increasing global loyalty. Needless to say, disarmament treaties will need the threat of sanctions for noncompliance.

We need church leaders to call unacceptable (1) that any nation promote its foreign policy goals through the sale and transfer of weapons, and (2) that arms of any kind be sold for commercial profit. It is shocking that military deterrence today should be directed primarily not against a foreign enemy but against domestic unemployment, a situation that could have been avoided had the need for conversion to a peacetime economy been anticipated by more than the peace community. Rarely has the latter been ahead of its time; it is only on time, with the rest of the country *behind* time. Just as the first step toward the abolition of slavery was the abolition of the slave trade, so now the first step toward the eventual abolition of national military arsenals should be the abolition of the arms trade. Sellers must be held as culpable as buyers. The United Nations should immediately begin to monitor and publicize all sales and transfers of arms from one country to another.

As conventional weapons are conventional only in the sense of being nonnuclear, hardly nonlethal, wars henceforth should be defined not by the weapons used but by the harm done. And as the harm done by conventional weapons is morally so reprehensible, Christians should be prepared to resist all reasons advanced for waging war. It should be clear to them that to fight merely for national honor or national interests is an act of religious infidelity. When religion is used to undergird militarism, then, like the man on the road from Jerusalem to Jericho, our faith has fallen among thieves who have stripped it of its meaning.

To save the environment—a second common task—we need an earth covenant, a form of Magna Carta for the earth. Such a charter would expand the Universal Declaration of Human Rights so that some of the ethical considerations that presently govern human relations will be extended to nature as well. In religious terms, we need to reconnect nature with nature's God, with a focus more "cosmocentric" than anthropocentric. With Native Americans, we need to recognize our spiritual tie with every leaf and creature; with Orthodox Christians, to see ourselves not only as stewards but as "priests of creation."

And, third, we need to go beyond charity. Charity is a matter of personal attributes, justice a matter of public policy. Never can the first be a substitute for the second.

Here in America and in the third world, the "haves" today have more than ever, while the "have-nots" are more numerous and more undeniably miserable. If people have equal dignity, there cannot be such degrees of economic inequality. As William Penn wrote: "It is a reproach to religion and government to suffer so much poverty and excess."

Communism in Eastern Europe failed in large part because it did not produce enough. But capitalism in the United States fails to share equitably the greater wealth it produces. Christians need to remember that privilege is often a matter of theft, that not only poverty but also superabundance can keep people in a subhuman state. And, of course, in their greed and quest for power both communism and capitalism have proved devastating to the environment.

In subsequent chapters I shall try to show how the three great causes of disarmament, ecology, and social justice are inextricably linked, and that only by serving the first—disarmament—can sufficient funds be saved to serve the other two.

Let me close this chapter with a final thought. I have urged the need to chip away at national sovereignty and expand global loyalty. But I believe that global loyalty will be reached through patriotism, not by rejecting it. Christians simply cannot allow political leaders to hijack patriotism in the service of fervent jingoism. As I see it, there are three kinds of patriots, two bad, one good. The bad patriots are the uncritical lovers and the loveless critics of their country. The good patriots are those who carry on a lover's quarrel with their country, a reflection of God's eternal lover's quarrel with the entire world.

Nationalism at the expense of another nation is as evil as racism at the expense of another race. Nevertheless, just as husbands can love their wives without denigrating other women, so patriots ought to be able to love their country without disparaging others. I love America, and it is precisely because I love my country and want to promote her best interests that I want her citizens to recognize their interdependence with all nations, their need for common rather than national security, the worldwide need for disarmament, environmental protection, and greater economic justice.

Genuine love expands, it doesn't contract. True patriotism can only extend minds and hearts, extend them to the point where all citizens in every land will one day vote for a vision of human unity once so eloquently described by a candidate for no less a post than that of the U.S. presidency: "We travel together, passengers on a little spaceship, dependent on its vulnerable supplies of air and soil; all committed for our safety to its security and peace, preserved from annihilation only by the care, the work, and I will say, the love we give our fragile craft" (Adlai Stevenson).

To eyes that are open, this vision is still accessible, not yet beyond hand's reach.

2

BEYOND WAR

"For every boot of the tramping warrior
in battle tumult
    and every garment rolled in blood
will be burned as fuel for the fire.
For to us a child is born
    To us a son is given." *Isaiah 9:5–6a*

"And so to the end of history, murder shall breed murder, always in the name of right and honor and peace, until at last the gods tire of blood and create a race that can understand."
G.B. Shaw, Caesar and Cleopatra

"War is a coward's escape from the problems of peace."
Thomas Mann

"The fourth is freedom from fear, which translated into world terms means a world-wide reduction of armaments to such a point that no nation will be in a position to commit an act of physical aggression against any neighbor—anywhere in the world."
Franklin Delano Roosevelt, January 1941

"If I could have three wishes, world peace would be all three."
Marlia, 8th grade

A SINGLE BURNING MATCH can today conflagrate the world. Why is that simple fact so hard to face? For an answer, let's return for a moment to Michelangelo's *Last Judgment* and to the notion that hell is truth seen too late. The primary reason for such blindness is that there is a basic unacceptability about unpleasant truth. We shield ourselves from its wounding accuracy. And if this is so of individuals, it's even truer of nations. Recall the biblical priest Amaziah and how, 2,700 years ago, he said of Amos the prophet, "The land is not able to bear all his words."[1]

Amaziah was no fool. He knew that none love you for being the enemy of their illusions. He knew that most people want peace at any price, as long as the peace is theirs and someone else pays the price. Inveighing against false prophets who tell people only what they want to hear, not what they need to know, Jeremiah describes them as having "treated the wound of my people carelessly,/saying, 'Peace, peace,'/when there is no peace."[2] And Jesus said: "Do not think that I have come to bring peace to the earth; I have not come to bring peace, but a sword."[3] He could

---

1. Amos 7:10.
2. Jeremiah 6:14.
3. Matthew 10:34.

only have meant the sword of truth, the only sword to heal the wounds it inflicts.

Perhaps no area of thought is more fraught with illusions than our thinking about national security. Few policies lag farther behind changes in reality than do military strategies. To illustrate the point, and to help prevent the repetition of some horrendous mistakes, let us first rehearse briefly the recent Soviet-American arms race. Then let's consider what might help to move the world beyond war.

I don't want to argue about who started the Cold War. The blame for it can certainly be widely shared and, given the interventions of the Soviet Union in Eastern Europe, Asia, and Africa, there was a justifiable need in the West for a policy of deterrence. But the extent of the arms buildup needs seriously to be challenged. It made common sense blush. It became an orgy, or more accurately a binge, with both sides behaving like alcoholics who know that liquor is killing them but who can always find a reason for one more drink.

Over the years American Presidents always sounded as if they were determined to end the arms race. President Eisenhower, in his address to the UN in 1953, called on the superpowers to "begin to diminish the potential destructive power of the world's atomic stockpiles."

President Kennedy, in the fall of 1961, warned that "mankind must put an end to war, or war will put an end to mankind. The risks in disarmament pale in comparison to the risks inherent in an unlimited arms race."

President Johnson, when he signed the Non-Proliferation of Nuclear Weapons Treaty in 1968, pledged that Washington and Moscow would "pursue negotiations in good faith for the cessation of the nuclear arms race."

President Nixon, in 1970, said that "the nuclear era places upon the two preponderant powers a unique responsibility to explore means of limiting military competition."

President Carter, in his Inaugural Address, expressed the hope that "nuclear weapons would be rid from the face of the earth."

But the desire to negotiate, continually affirmed on both sides, was never accompanied by a willingness to disarm. Arms control meant control up, never down. While Secretary of Defense McNamara in the 1960s talked of "sufficiency," his successors stressed superiority; not "When is enough?" but "Who's ahead?" There was much talk of the need for "bargaining chips," but they proved all chips, no bargains. No one in government seemed to realize that historically buildups don't lead to reductions, only to matching buildups by the other side. By accepting a nuclear arms race as an unchangeable fact, Soviet and American leaders helped to perpetuate it, even though its continuation inexorably decreased rather than increased the national security of every nation on earth. It is no exaggeration to say that the two superpowers played Russian roulette with the world, all the while spurning offers of mediation. The so-called Five Continent Peace Initiative, consisting of the leaders of Mexico, Argentina, Sweden, Tanzania, and India, warned that "The whole world has become as a prisoner in a cell, condemned to death, awaiting the uncertain moment of execution."

By the late 1980s the United States and the USSR together had some fifty thousand nuclear warheads, enough to take out everyone in the world about seventeen times over. The explosive power of fifty thousand nuclear warheads is such that if one Hiroshima-size bomb were to be dropped every minute—sixty bombs an hour—the bombing would continue uninterrupted for two solid years.

The economic price tag was enormous. In 1983, when looking for some light reading, I came across this paragraph in an airplane magazine.

A Trident submarine costs 1.7 billion dollars. But that's only one submarine. Let's talk a trillion. For one trillion dollars, you could build a $75,000 house, place it on $5,000 worth of land, furnish it with $10,000 worth of furniture, put a $10,000 car in the garage and give all this to each and every family in Kansas, Missouri, Nebraska, Oklahoma, Colorado and Iowa. Having done this, you would still have enough left to build a 10 million dollar hospital and a 10 million dollar library in each of 250 cities and towns throughout the six-state region. After having done all that, you would still have enough money left to build 500 schools at 10 million dollars each for the communities in the region, and after having done all that you would still have enough left out of the original trillion to put aside, at ten percent annual interest, a sum of money that would pay a salary of $25,000 per year for an army of ten thousand nurses, the same salary for an army of ten thousand teachers and an annual cash allowance of $5,000 for each and every family throughout the six-state region—not just for one year, but forever.

(Republic Airlines Magazine)

To put the trillion in perspective, remember that one trillion dollars was only one half of what the Reagan administration spent on military budgets alone.

The spiritual price tag was even higher. Probably the best word on the Cold War was spoken centuries ago by Saint Augustine, who said, "Imagine the vanity of thinking that your enemy can do you more damage than your enmity."

The Cold War was devastating to warm hearts. The divine commandment to love your enemy was changed into an imperative to hate all Communists. Hatred became a patriotic virtue. We became more and more ignorant of things we were most assured. President Reagan actually said, "Let us not delude ourselves, the Soviet Union underlies all the unrest that is going on. If they weren't engaged in this game of dominoes, there wouldn't be any hot spots in the world."

To believe that dominoes fall only from outside pressure, never from inner weakness, is to believe that all riots in American cities are caused by outside agitators.

Bearing out Augustine's point, and as if in anticipation of Cold War relations, the poet Yeats wrote:

> We had fed the heart on fantasies,
> The heart's grown brutal from the fare;
> More substance in our enmities
> Than in our love.

In the preceding chapter I discussed the immediate need for a comprehensive test ban, the need to ban the worldwide trade of all arms, and eventually to assemble international peacekeeping forces larger than any national force.

Regarding nuclear disarmament, Rajiv Gandhi had this to say to the UN special session on disarmament in 1988: "History is full of myths parading as iron laws of science: that the white race is superior to colored races, that women are inferior to men, that colonization is a civilizing mission, and that nations that have nuclear weapons are responsible powers while those that do not, are not."

What Gandhi understood so well was that just as a fat person cannot talk persuasively to a skinny one about the virtues of not overeating, so nuclear powers cannot convince nonnuclear ones to renounce access to nuclear weapons—not until the nuclear powers themselves start seriously to disarm. Either they disarm, or they must face the fact that any nation in the world that wants nuclear weapons eventually will get them. Either the world becomes nuclear-free, or the whole planet becomes a nuclear porcupine.

Finally, let me point out that even if, by the grace of God, we succeed in ridding the earth of weapons of mass destruction, the ability to make them will forever and ever be part of the storehouse of human knowledge. Of all thoughts about the world's future, few are more sobering, for it would be utterly naive to believe that a nation at war would gracefully choose to go down to defeat rather than reconstruct nuclear weapons had it the ability to do so. In other words, having bitten the nuclear apple there is no returning to innocence. It's hard not to conclude that humanity has outlived war—but doesn't know it.

The New Testament records three major temptations of Christ. In the second (see Luke, chapter 4) the devil takes Jesus up to a high place and, after showing him "in an instant all the kingdoms of the world," says to him, "To you I will give their glory and all this authority; for it has been given over to me." (A view of the world too accurate for comfort!) Then the devil makes his proposal: "If you, then, will worship me, it will all be yours."

What is the temptation if not the ancient but timeless one of seeking status through power? The sin of Adam and Eve had nothing to do with sex, everything to do with power. True, their disobedient deed took place at the foot of the tree of knowledge, but it was hardly for the sake of knowledge that Adam and Eve took the apple. They wanted power; they wanted to know more, to have more, to be more. "You will be like God" (Gen. 3:5) tempted the serpent, and they jumped at the chance, as to this day does the Adam or Eve in almost every one of us. (If not literally true, the story is eternally true).

If the temptation was serious to Jesus, and almost irresistible to us, we can be sure that to seek status through power is a thoroughly irresistible temptation to a superpower. And that's why for years we Americans went on arming—way beyond sufficiency, far beyond what any strategy of deterrence required. That's why in 1953 our CIA overthrew the duly elected government of Iran, and the following year the duly elected government of Guatemala. That's why we propped up dictators like Marcos and Diem, and killed rulers like Lumumba, assuming for ourselves a right we would never accord others—the right to decide who lives, dies, and rules in third-world countries. And that's why so many of our leaders today want to see to it that the United States remains the sole superpower of the world.

As always, the stated goal is lofty, this time to provide stability in a volatile world. But if we look at our patterns of action, our basic interests, and our power relations, we have to conclude that just as before, so now our primary concern is to preserve a status quo favorable to us. We are far more concerned with disorder than with injustice. And nations more concerned with disorder than injustice invariably produce more of both. Said Amos to such nations, "You think to defer the day of misfortune, but you hasten the reign of violence."[4]

More clearly than most other institutions, churches should see that it is our pride-swollen faces that close up our eyes, that no nation is well served by illusions of its righteousness. All nations make decisions based on self-interest and then defend them in the name of morality. Saint Augustine gave excellent advice not only to individuals but to nations as well when he said, "Never fight evil as if it were something that arose totally outside of yourself." He was reflecting Saint Paul's "all have sinned and fallen short."[5] It is tempting, of course, to believe that some have sinned—for example, "that evil empire"—or that "most have sinned, but not us." Paul's insistence, however, that "*all* have sinned" makes an important point: if we are not one with

---

4. Amos 6:3.
5. Romans 3:23.

our enemies in love, at least we are one with them in sin, which is no mean bond, for it precludes the possibility of separation through judgment. That is the meaning of the injunction "Judge not, that ye be not judged."[6]

Innocence may be beguiling in children, but it is spiritually disastrous in adults, who ought to know that in the sullied stream of human life it is not innocence but holiness that is our only option. As with individuals, so with nations, their salvation lies not in being sinless but in believing that there is more mercy in God than sin in us.

We are now living in the morning of a new age. With the Cold War over and the Soviet Union gone, there is no reason for the United States and the world not to proceed apace with disarmament. Power now is rooted more in economic than in military strength. Unlike the bipolar world of yesterday, the future will be multipolar, the danger being a multipolar free-for-all. But in any event, the United States will no longer be the superpower it was, and that's nothing to brood, stew, and seethe over, for what Ezekiel said of Tyre is true of us: "You corrupted your wisdom for the sake of your splendor."[7]

Said de Tocqueville, "America is great because America is good. If she ceases to be good, she ceases to be great." With less power, we Americans will be better able to be good, both to ourselves and to others. I have great confidence in America. We are still a young country, with lots of raw energy. We're a country of immigrants, whose sons and daughters still harbor a love for the impossible task. Yet we must change the national imagination, shed our self-righteousness, rid ourselves of our macho love of weapons inherited from our macho frontier past. It is time now to honor the countless Americans who have died in wars they shouldn't have been asked to fight, wars that

6. Matthew 7:1.
7. Ezekiel 28:17.

might have been avoided, settled by negotiations—honor them by putting an end to the vainglory, the blunderings, and the carnage that cost them their lives.

American churches can contribute enormously by seeing how pathologically dysfunctional war is rapidly becoming. Let them affirm the psalmist's contention that "the war horse is a vain hope for victory, and by its great might it cannot save."[8] Churches have a special obligation to point out that "God'n'country" is not one word, and to summon America to a higher vision of its meaning and destiny.

Churches all over the world must see to it that non-violence becomes a strategy not only for individuals and groups, but one taught governments. If arms reductions are to become more likely and wars less so, then new measures have to be devised for conflict resolution. The upkeep for international peacekeeping forces should be charged right now to national defense budgets, and such forces should be assigned to borders before a conflict begins, not only when it ends. Mediation must become the order of the day. Every nation should abandon its claim to be a judge in its own cause. Nations must learn to listen to one another, to affirm the valid interests of adversaries, to cease judgmental propaganda, to heed international law. We must replace the concept of national security with that of common security, an understanding that the security of countries cannot be imagined separately, for none is really secure until all are secure.

Obviously, inhuman behavior is not about to disappear, and the mass media have made it all but impossible to hide mass murders and mass starvation. No longer can any of us say, "I didn't know"—whether the destruction of life takes place across borders or within borders. To deal with

8. Psalms 33:17.

the latter we need to devise legitimate international ways to counter the worst depredations of nationalism, tribalism, and racism. I have in mind the horrors of Idi Amin and Pol Pot, the starvation of Somalians and Serbian "ethnic cleansing." Moral isolation is not an acceptable alternative. for those opposed to war. The issue of humanitarian interventions to protect basic human rights looms large. It must be faced, and the solutions we find will go a long way toward defining who we are and "the new world order."

The eventual size, shape, command, and authority of a genuine international police force is hard today to perceive. What is clear is that henceforth nations are called to confer, not conquer, to discuss, not destroy, to extend olive branches, not their missile ranges. The new era already upon us reminds us that God is not mocked: we have to be merciful when we live at each other's mercy; we have to learn to be meek or there will be no earth to inherit.

3

THE ENVIRONMENT

"The heavens are telling the glory of God;
   and the firmament proclaims his handiwork."
Psalm 19:1

"O! pardon me, thou bleeding piece of earth,
   That I am meek and gentle with these butchers!"
William Shakespeare, Julius Caesar

"Whatever befalls the earth befalls the sons of earth. Man
did not weave the web of life; he is merely a strand in it.
Whatever he does to the web, he does to himself. . . .
Continue to contaminate your bed and you will one night
suffocate in your own waste."

Chief Seattle, 1854

"We sit astride the world like some military dictator, some
smelly Papa Doc."

Bill McKibben

WHILE THE HEAVENS CONTINUE TO TELL the glory of God, the firmament today also proclaims some nefarious human handiwork—smog, acid rain, an immense hole in the ozone layer. Fortunately, since the first Earth Day in 1970, ecology has become a household word and environmental affairs a popular college major. Fortunately, too, more and more Americans are beginning to realize that the average American car driven the average American distance—10,000 miles a year—releases annually into the atmosphere its own weight in carbon.

The danger to the entire earth is immense. Scientists tell us that in the last three decades, carbon dioxide in the atmosphere has increased more than 10 percent. Since 1985 the damage to German forests caused by acid rain, the result of sulphur dioxide from burning fossil fuels, has risen from 10 percent to 50 percent; in Sweden, all bodies of fresh water are now acidic; from 1964 to 1979, acid rain killed half the mid- to high-elevation spruce trees in the state of Vermont, while one Tennessee's–worth of the Amazonian rain forest is slashed and burned each year. As apparently there are more different species of birds in each square mile of that rain forest than exist in all of North America, we are silencing songs we have never even heard.

Then there is the "population bomb," as Paul Ehrlich in 1968 described the increasing rate of world population growth. It took a thousand years for the population of the world to double to 500 million in 1650. Then it doubled again, in only two hundred years, to 1 billion. The next doubling took only eighty years. Then, from 1930 to 1992— a mere sixty-two years—world population has gone from 2 billion to 5 1/2 billion, with 6 billion anticipated by 1998.

Obviously, if we double energy efficiency but double also the number of energy users, we accomplish little. Unless significant corrective measures are quickly taken, it would appear that the entire human race is about to compound original sin with terminal sin.

Environmentalists sometimes accuse Christians and Jews of complicity in the destruction of the environment. They remind us that God told Adam to "have dominion over the fish of the sea and over the birds of the air and over every living thing that moves upon the earth."[1]

I doubt that the vast majority of all of us polluters have given a moment's thought to those words. The accusation is really another example of a very narrow reading of a very short biblical passage. When God also told Adam to "till [the garden] and keep it,"[2] God could hardly have had in mind the careless, unbridled subjugation and exploitation so clearly attributable to sinful greed.

A far more serious accusation is that Jews and Christians no longer see nature at one with nature's God. No longer are our actions inhibited by wonder. To be sure, in church and synagogue we recite the Nineteenth and other psalms in which God and nature are seen to be inseparable: "When I look at thy heavens, the work of thy fingers, the moon and stars which Thou has established . . . "[3] We sing

1. Genesis 1:28.
2. Genesis 2:15.
3. Psalm 8:3.

hymns based on these psalms, "The Spacious Firmament on High," "Joyful, Joyful, We Adore Thee." But our adoration does not extend in any meaningful way to God's creation. Like almost all Americans—Native Americans being a great exception—we have divorced nature from nature's God. We view nature essentially as a toolbox. Nature may have beauty but no purpose. It is there solely to serve human purposes.

I am convinced that unless in our own minds we rewed nature to nature's God, we are not going to save our environment. Caution lest we exhaust our natural resources and kill ourselves in the process—that kind of caution is not enough. What we need beyond caution is reverence. What we need beyond practical fears are moral qualms. Unless nature is "resanctified," we will never see nature as worthy of ethical considerations similar to those that presently govern human relations. And I'm not at all optimistic. For not only are Christians poor stewards of God's creation, seriously challenging the Christian notion of "stewardship" are those who want us to think of ourselves as planet managers. And management today includes biotechnology, genetic engineering, a way to create new life. In conceptual and moral terms, genetic engineering may well be the most important scientific advance since the smashing of the atom. It suggests that if nature can't put up with our numbers and habits, well, we'll just have to change nature. We'll create crops that can survive a much warmer climate, we'll alter human genes. And, of course, there's plenty of extra space in outer space where, as shuttle flights indicate, plants grow faster.

A lot of people are talking this kind of language. They are impatient with moral restraints. They rebuke us for panicking. They say we should be looking forward to our next "evolutionary exam." While I have many doubts about our passing this exam, I have few about our taking it.

Because medical cures, more and better food, as well as other good things, are bound to result from advances in biotechnology, it feels wrong to oppose its advance. But that's the way so many of us felt in the '50s when President Eisenhower extolled "atoms for peace." Few foresaw the way we would charge ahead with the production of nuclear power, with no real solution at hand or even in sight for the nuclear wastes that we're now told will be radioactive for 25,000 years.

Because proponents of genetic engineering are intrigued by nature's possibilities more than they revere nature itself, they display more hubris than humility. Theirs is a perilous undertaking. If Christians can't oppose it unconditionally, their spiritual qualms need very much to become part of the public dialogue. It has always been my hope that human beings might be clever enough to make things but wise enough to forgo doing so. Perhaps before funding any specific project in biotechnology, we should fund a study to consider the wisdom of it. Personally, I find compelling the words of Dennis Hayes, chairperson of Earth Day 1990. "The most fundamental human truth," he said, "is that although we humans routinely violate our own laws, we can't break Nature's laws. We can only prove them."

Far less complex and today more urgent is the need to start implementing something like Vice President Albert Gore's "Marshall Plan" for saving the planet. From 1948 to 1951 the Marshall Plan cost close to 2 percent of United States' GNP. A similar percentage today would be almost $100 billion a year. Our total nonmilitary foreign aid budget is presently about $15 billion a year, hardly comparable. But the need for a new Marshall Plan is altogether as great as was the need for the old.

We must, of course, stabilize world population and prevent famine. But it is simplistic to say that hunger results only from too many mouths to feed. China, for example, has more people than any other country. Yet in 1985 China produced enough grain to send surplus amounts to Ethiopia. In Holland where there are three hundred people per square kilometer, there is no starvation.

Blaming overpopulation also ignores the need for large families. With no social security or pensions, our ancestors too had large families—enough hands to work the land and care for the home. Family planning in those days meant large families, as today it still does in third-world countries. Actually there is more than enough food to feed everyone. The trouble is, those who need it most can afford it least.

To increase food production in third-world countries, Gore and other experts underscore the need for literacy and education emphasizing simple techniques in sustainable agriculture, lessons to prevent soil erosion, planting trees, cleansing wells and streams. Extremely important is reducing infant mortality, for, as Julius Nyerere once remarked, "the most powerful contraceptive is the confidence by parents that their children will survive."

Obviously birth-control devices need everywhere to be available. In America it is important to recognize that the vast majority of those opposing abortion do not object to contraception. It is only to hold together their political coalition that they do not challenge the few who do. With a little more honesty Americans could help expedite the stabilization of world population.

To save the environment, Gore advances an "SEI,"—a Strategic Environment Initiative—to deal in America with waste reduction, recycling, conservation of soil, forestry, and energy. It is technologically possible today to construct cars that would go five times as many miles to a gallon of fuel, and to run on photovoltaic cells. Also, a single new energy-saving bulb, compared to a standard bulb, saves a ton of coal over its lifetime. And if storm runoff water in every city could be separated from waste water, sewage treatments wouldn't be so overwhelmed as to dump sewage into rivers and lakes.

Following an earlier suggestion of former Soviet foreign minister Shevardnadze, Vice President Gore advocates an Environmental Security Council for the United Nations. Its primary purpose would be to share and stimulate the development of appropriate technologies, the kind that don't destroy the environment. Such a council could spawn a whole new generation of treaties and agreements such as the Montreal Protocol, adopted in 1987, which sought to reduce the amounts of CFCs and related chemicals in the atmosphere, and the Earth Summit in 1992 in Rio de Janeiro.

It is a great mistake to talk, as many political leaders do, of balancing the needs of the economy with those of the environment. Any economy, national or world, is a subsystem of the ecosystem. Therefore we cannot speak of growth as an unquestioned good. National banks and the World Bank should fund only such development projects as are ecologically sound. American industries should provide executive compensation for environmental stewardship as the enlightened among them still reward results in affirmative action.

I would love, with the wave of a wand, to declare the solar age "open," for solar energy is living off income, fossil fuel off savings. When you think that the vast majority of poor people live in the southern tier of this planet—in Central and Latin America, in Africa and Asia—and that the one thing they all have in abundance is sunshine, it breaks your heart that we have poured so many of our resources into weapons research and so few into the development of what eventually will be for billions of poor people a cheap, benign, and endlessly renewable source of energy.

America must convince itself that emergency measures require immediate implementation. If indeed we are stewards of God's creation, Christians have a big role to play. And the results could be dramatic, for the environmental point of view turns us away from the possessive individualism that has long been our secular credo and toward the interdependency that alone can save us. It was one thing for people to consume nature's surpluses. Today we are destroying the productive base of both present and future surpluses. Only together, all together, can we save that base. Only together can we eliminate toxic wastes in the atmosphere. Only together can we engage in the serious disarmament that will spring loose the funds to fight pollution. And because saving the environment is an enterprise so positive and so inclusive, its success is sure to help make the military impulse look ever more neurotic.

An ugly truth stares us in the face. Let us not wait until it hits us in the face. The churches are morally obligated to develop a focus, energy, and resolve to save the environment. Most of all, they can rewed nature to nature's God, for only reverence can restrain our violence toward nature. It is primarily our lack of wonder that prevents our foreseeing and forestalling the havoc we will leave in our wake. In this "age of information" let us remember that "the greater the island of knowledge the greater the shoreline of wonder" (Huston Smith). Let us recall G.K. Chesterton's observation: "The world does not lack for wonders, only for a sense of wonder." Without wonder, we'll never save life on the planet. God, I'm sure, approves e.e. cumming's preference:

> I would rather learn from one bird how to sing
> than teach ten thousand stars how not to dance.

4

BEYOND CHARITY

"I would like to love my country and still love justice."
Albert Camus

"Justice is sorting out what belongs to whom and returning it to them."
Walter Brueggemann

"Property: the more common it is, the holier it is."
Saint Gertrude

"Let justice roll down like waters,
and righteousness like an
ever-flowing stream."
Amos 5:24

"The future of God is the future of the poor.
Dorothee Soelle

AN OLD SAYING HOLDS that religion and politics don't mix. Probably it was first said by Pharaoh when he turned down Moses' plea to "let my people go." Generally what it means is, "Your religion doesn't mix with my politics." When the right-wing press of Latin America, for example, accused the progressive Brazilian bishop F. Helda Camara of mixing religion and politics, he replied, "When the Roman Catholic Church was everywhere in bed with military juntas, you never accused us of mixing religion and politics."

If religion is where it all comes together—the microcosm and the macrocosm, intimate relationships and public policy—if Christians are called so to live "that in everything God may be glorified,"[1] then religion and politics do mix and to claim otherwise is really to understand neither.

But to claim they mix is not to say they are identical. It is one thing to say with the prophet, "Let justice roll down like mighty waters,"[2] and quite another to work out the irrigation system. The former is a religious concern, the latter a political task.

---

1. 1 Peter 4:11.
2. Amos 5:24.

While Christians certainly don't have to take positions on every issue, on matters of justice they have no choice. Said South African bishop Desmond Tutu, "When the elephant has his foot on the tail of the mouse, and you say you are neutral, the mouse will not appreciate your neutrality."

And neither will God. Remember God's words to Moses: "I have seen the affliction of my people in Egypt; and have heard their cry. . . .Come, I will send you to Pharaoh that you may bring forth the children of Israel out of Egypt."[3] When you stop to think about it, how can God be neutral? How can God do otherwise than side with the oppressed? If God sided with tyrants, God would be malevolent. If God sided with no one, God would be indifferent, which is to say again "malevolent," because God would be supporting tyranny by not protesting it.

The story of God and Moses and Pharaoh reminds us that compassion, for its implementation, demands confrontation. It also puts churches on notice to identify not with the structures of power but with the victims of power.

I said in the first chapter that charity was a matter of personal attributes while justice concerned public policy. Obviously the churches have to feed the hungry, clothe the naked, and shelter the homeless. But they have also to remember that the answer to homelessness is homes, not shelters. What the poor and downtrodden need is not piecemeal charity, but justice. And to show how charity can actually impede the progress of justice, Karl Marx once said to a group of church folk: "You Christians have a vested interest in unjust structures which produce victims, to whom you then can pour out your hearts in charity." His insight, of course, was biblical before it was Marxist, for biblical justice asks not only that we alleviate the effects of injustice, but that we eradicate the causes of it.

---

3. Exodus 3:7, 10.

When I was a boy in public school I was told that in America we have rich people and poor people, and there was no connection between them. Years later, in New York City, I often heard well-to-do people say that while New York was the adrenaline capital of the world, the most exciting city with the best of everything, "we also have problems—a lot of poor people." Reading the Bible, I found the problem defined differently. In the Bible, it's always the rich who are a problem to the poor, never the other way around. There are poor people *because* there are rich people, a connection Oscar Romero, the martyred Roman Catholic leader of El Salvador, never failed to make by calling the many poor in his country not *los pobres* but *los apobrecidos,* "the impoverished," those "made poor."

In the New Testament, wealthy people like Zacchaeus, Lazarus, and Joseph of Arimathea receive sympathetic treatment. Still, Jesus doesn't hesitate to generalize that it is harder for a rich person to enter the kingdom of heaven than for a camel to pass through the eye of a needle. To quote Helda Camara again: "I used to think when I was a child that Christ might have been exaggerating when he warned about the dangers of wealth. Today I know better. I know how hard it is to be rich and still keep the milk of human kindness. Money has a dangerous way of freezing peoples' hands, eyes, lips, and hearts."

It is very hard to convert the heart, mind, and purse. It is very hard to have possessions and not become possessive, to be completely dependent upon God and independent of everything else. So, a prophetic concern for the poor should be matched by a pastoral concern for the rich. As I read the Bible, judgment against the rich spells mercy not only for the poor, but finally for the rich as well. It suggests that just as the poor should not be left at the mercy of their poverty, so the rich should not be left at the mercy of their wealth. If a minimum wage is just, there's more than symmetry to commend a maximum wage. After all, the primary reward for a job well done is not a higher salary but greater responsibilities.

There is an enormous difference between justice in our country and justice elsewhere. In Sweden, for instance, chief executive officers as a general rule make no more than six times the salary of their lowest paid employee. There is also, I'm told, a continuing debate with conservatives arguing for a seven to one ratio, while radicals urge a five to one ratio. In America it's sometimes four hundred to one and no debate!

One of the attributes of power is that it gives those who have it the ability to define reality and the power to make others believe in their definition. Thus it is that private property in America has come to be considered all but sacred. Obviously this makes its redistribution difficult, even through taxation. Churchgoers have often heard the psalmist's contention that "the earth is the Lord's and all that is in it,"[4] and readers of Job will recall God's informing him that "whatever is under the whole heaven is mine."[5] In other words, from a religious point of view, God is the landlord of ultimate title. It was that understanding that led Pope Paul VI to say: "Private property does not constitute for anyone an absolute and unconditional right. No one is justified in keeping for his exclusive use what he does not need, when others lack necessities" (*Populorum Progressio*). If I read him correctly, the pope is saying that sharing our surplus is an act of justice rather than an act of benevolence.

But to dispute the sacredness of private property is not to deny its validity. "Thou shalt not steal," "Thou shalt not covet": implicitly and explicitly the Ten Commandments sanction private property, and throughout scripture the

4. Psalm 24:1.
5. Job 41:11.

legitimacy of private property is affirmed. How, for instance, could Jesus command his followers to give to the poor or to loan without hope of repayment unless they had sufficient funds to make such gifts and loans? And even the saints, who renounced their worldly goods, often made a distinction between poverty and destitution.

As regards private property, and as the pope's statement makes clear, the question of ownership is subordinate to the question of use. It was that moral understanding that finally led to laws in this country that stipulated that African Americans be admitted in privately owned restaurants, that Jews be included in heretofore Gentile fraternities, and women in formerly all-men's clubs.

I know that the earliest Christians "had all things in common."[6] But subsequent Christian communes, like many a kibbutz in Israel, found the ideal beyond the capacity of frail mortals. It strikes me that private property is much like the garments of skin with which the Lord thoughtfully clothed Adam and Eve. In a perfect world, unlimited intimacy would hold no dangers, all property could safely be held in common, and there would be no exploitation. But in a fallen world, to protect us from exploitation, we need our own homes, our own "turf"; we need a little distance between us. We are distanced, however, not to keep us apart, but to facilitate our coming together. Like the garments of skin, and for that matter all clothing, if private property enhances our life together, then it is good; if it pushes us yet farther apart, it is bad. In other words, private property is justified not by the precariousness of our individual lives, but by the fragility of our common life. And that is what is being torn apart today in America. Never in all our national history has the gap between rich and poor been as wide as it is today, despite our pledge of allegiance to a nation "with liberty *and justice* for all" (italics added).

---

6. Acts 2:44.

The United States has known three gilded ages: the 1890s, the 1920s, and the 1980s. These were ages marked by a gaudy orgy of getting and spending, times when avarice was counted a good thing, a sign of social fitness. How much the three ages resemble one another is illustrated by the Populist platform issued just over one hundred years ago, on July 2, 1892. The Populists declared they were meeting "in the midst of a nation brought to the verge of moral, political and material ruin. Corruption dominates the ballot-box, the Legislatures, the Congress, and touches even the ermine of the bench. The fruits of the toil of millions are boldly stolen to build up colossal fortunes for a few. . . . From the same prolific womb of governmental injustice we breed the two great classes— tramps and millionaires."

Ninety years later, President Reagan announced: "What I want to see above all is that this remains a country where someone can always get rich." With little concern for who got poor, and with the obvious consent of congressional Democrats, President Reagan combined tax cuts for the rich with spending cuts for the poor. The result was a massive upward redistribution of wealth, which saw the incomes of the top 10 percent of the population rise by 74 percent, while those of the bottom 10 percent fell 10.5 percent. The fortunate top fifth took home more money than the other four fifths put together. If they thought about it, the Christians among them must have had a hard time squaring their take-home pay with the remembrance that Christ's sole possession at death was a robe!

During the Reagan years in New York City I watched the decay of everything not connected with profit-making— schools, libraries, hospitals, roads, bridges, even the public monuments. "Enrich thyself" was the clarion call. It was right to buy, wrong to defer almost any gratification. While the "permissiveness" of the 1960s was frequently attacked, consumerism in the '80s was never included in the condemnation. Night after night, fancy restaurants teemed with Wall Street traders spending money like rajas and sheikhs, while parks and other public places filled with the homeless.

The upshot was that the rich, in effect, forsook their stake in the common life of the nation. Economist and now Secretary of Labor Robert Reich wrote of "the secession of the successful." He pointed out that as the rich abandoned public services—parks, schools, hospitals— these lost their advocates. It was little wonder that schools became holding bins, that parks were abandoned to purveyors of drugs, that public hospitals concealed the homeless, the mentally disturbed and contagiously ill—those, we should add, not discharged to the streets.

Barbara Ehrenreich summarized the situation: "The uphill financial climb of the rich accelerates the downward spiral of society as a whole," leading to widening inequalities, heightened estrangement, and "the moral amnesia that estrangement requires."

The '80s were a perfect example of the biblical contention that it is the rich who are a problem to the poor. The rich simply couldn't get richer without the poor getting poorer—not when opportunity counted for so much more than equality. As Republican commentator Kevin Phillips analyzed it, there was "new wealth in profusion for the bright, the bold, the educated and politically favored." For those less fortunate, it was "economic carnage."

During the 1980s we were a country of ostriches, a whole society in denial. Happily, the artificial optimism of the decade has now lost its luster. There is growing consensus that America must be rebuilt, although how best to do it is much disputed.

There is no question that the churches can help; the question is whether they will. They will if they see justice as central to, not ancillary to, the gospel; if they understand that the gospel is good news to the poor or it is not good news at all. They will if, recalling the story of God, Moses, and Pharaoh, they remember that God's strategy is less to sensitize the powerful than to empower the powerless.

Following the lead of Oscar Romero, Christians must see the poor as "the impoverished," those made poor by a shortage of housing and jobs, by health and educational systems rampant with inequalities, and by a market system often kinder to companies than to people. If property is not sacred, you can be sure no market system is either. If "the sabbath was made for humankind"[7] the economy belongs to human beings.

Let Christians challenge the rest of the nation, not try to resemble the rest of the nation. Let them proclaim the biblical norms for justice that give primary emphasis not to accomplishment, but to need. There is no reason why the well-to-do should begrudge the checks that allow the elderly and the disabled to live better. Why should a nation resent the free medical care that allows poor mothers and their children to see doctors more often? When Congress created a food-stamp program, recipients not only ate better, but had a little money to spend on other things. When Congress subsidized Section 8 housing, families fortunate enough to get a certificate lived in somewhat nicer apartments and paid far less rent. Without question, many poor have many vices, mostly those that go with powerlessness or poverty. But it is outrageous to pretend that families can make do on the sums that welfare currently provides them. Welfare is a hypocritical system that forces its recipients to engage in fraud. Most welfare mothers try to find extra money not because they like to cheat, but because they love their children. And most stay on welfare not because

---

7. Mark 2:27.

they like it, but because in most communities there are more unskilled workers than unskilled jobs and very few programs to train people for jobs that pay more.

It is also a gross exaggeration to say there is no money for antipoverty programs. Military cutbacks alone could range from $250 billion to $400 billion over the next five years. The restoration of a progressive income tax would raise revenues we presently squander on the wealthy. We could raise the top rate paid by the wealthiest taxpayers (38 percent doesn't seem unreasonable if 40 percent wasn't unreasonable in England under Margaret Thatcher), reduce mortgage-interest deductions for the wealthy, increase luxury taxes, and close estate and gift tax loopholes and corporate tax loopholes as well, particularly those of multinational corporations.

In the long run it's cheaper to eradicate poverty than to maintain it. Every year we pay huge sums for poverty in crime and prison construction, in output lost because of unemployment. And, as Teresa Amott has written, "Ending poverty would not only save us money; it might save our souls."

In American political history, the central question has always been, do you enhance the economic prospects for the many, or safeguard the accumulated wealth of the few? And the problem has never really been the "haves" vs. the "have-nots"; it has been between the "have-too-much" and the "have-too-little." Roosevelt stated it well in 1939: "Progress is not measured by how much we add to the abundance of those who already have a great deal, but by how much we do for those who have too little." Surely Christians would agree that it is better to multiply the loaves and the fishes for all than to make a larger, tastier dinner for the few.

I have chosen to talk only of our domestic economic situation because a nation's foreign policy, to a degree rarely recognized, reflects its attitude toward its domestic problems. In the 1980s our foreign aid to third-world countries helped the rich get richer, the poor get poorer, and the military become more powerful. No one should have been surprised; it was a perfect reflection of what was going on at home. If, in the years ahead, well-to-do Americans come to see their own complicity in the plight of the poor, come to understand them more than they presently fear them, if they accord the poor at home the respect and help that is their due, such efforts will surely strengthen our resolve, in concert with other nations, to see fulfilled, the world around, all hopes for justice so long and cruelly deferred.

5

RACE AND CLASS

"Those who make peaceful evolution impossible make
violent revolution inevitable."

John F. Kennedy

"If you have come to help me you can go home again.
But if you see my struggle as part of your own survival,
then perhaps we can work together."

*From Aboriginal Australian Delegation to Manila,
Declaration on People's Participation
and Sustainable Development*

Carl Sandburg was asked, "What is the ugliest word in
the English language?" After much thought, his answer:
"Exclusive."

AMERICANS ARE PRONE TO BE FAIR, but that's not the same thing as aching for justice. Likewise, believing as almost all of us do, that "all people are created equal" is not the same as feeling the monstrosity of inequality. For whatever reason—be it the blindness of sightless souls, the indifference of distracted people, or just plain compassion fatigue—whatever the reasons, the majority of white Americans do not feel the monstrosity of inequality so universally felt today by black Americans. The result is that racism remains bone-deep in American society.

Typically, white Americans feel that segregation was part of an evil era now over and gone and that, in any event, they themselves don't discriminate. Such thinking, of course, is dangerous: like rivers, we carry with us the silt of our past, and even a touch of bigotry is a touch of sin.

Typically, white Americans think black Americans today are getting something for nothing, and seeing it as their due. These white Americans, who love their history, want African Americans to forget theirs, to forget that after the Civil War Congress passed constitutional amendments, voting laws, and other statutes that were far stronger than those it passed in the 1960s and 1970s. The 1860s saw a black governor of Louisiana, a black majority in the South

Carolina legislature, black senators from Mississippi, and for the emancipated slaves electing them there was provided education and land—forty acres and a mule. It was inconceivable that people should be freed without the wherewithal to make their freedom real.

African Americans are today asking only for things that for the last hundred years have been theirs by virtue of a constitution that every congressional member and every American President are sworn to uphold. Small wonder that, along with Native Americans, they feel the United States government never quite lives up to anything it writes down.

Legal segregation, to be sure, has ended. But racial isolation has remained. The legal equality guaranteed once again in the 1950s, '60s and '70s was properly presumed to be a precursor of greater economic equality. So when school segregation in our larger cities is greater today than it was at the time of the 1954 *Brown v. Topeka Board of Education* decision, when unemployment, even among educated blacks, greatly exceeds that of their white counterparts, and when millions of African Americans—jobless, unskilled, and without hope—are seemingly trapped in a subculture of despair ready to crumble into violence at the slightest touch, it is clear that legal equality promised far more than it delivered.

Racism is a congenital deformity in our body politic. It is not, as Gunnar Myrdal in 1944 charitably called it, an "American Dilemma." It is *an American tragedy*. Racial discrimination is the one thing most clearly wrong with our country. In the eyes of the world it not only undermines our frequent claims to moral leadership, it contradicts everything our country stands for.

Since the 1960s, the number of college-educated African Americans has increased dramatically. But so too has the number of truly disadvantaged Americans, the rural as well as the urban poor, Native Americans, Hispanics, and Anglo-Americans, as well as African Americans. So we need to talk of poverty as well as prejudice, of class as well as race. And in such a sea of hardship and social ills, the churches have no business being withdrawn islands of piety. If we Christians can't get our social gospel back on track and implement it nonviolently, others will surely attempt it violently, and our failure will be the cause of it.

As I have often implied, the times beg for understanding. One way to seek it is to dethrone pseudo facts from their positions of infallibility. One of these is that the War on Poverty failed. The war didn't fail, it was President Johnson who failed. So preoccupied did he become with the war in Vietnam, the wrong war, the war eight thousand miles away, that he only declared but never really fought the right war here at home. But the blame is hardly his alone. In April 1985, Episcopal Bishop Paul Moore of New York City said:

> We once had a war against poverty; it is said to have failed. It failed only because the people of the United States lost their nerve and lost their way in the swamps of Vietnam and Watergate. If the war on poverty had been continued, restructured where necessary, monitored for corruption where appropriate, and encouraged with resources where successful, hunger would not have reappeared on the American scene, the homeless would not now walk the streets, and the schools would not fail to prepare youths for jobs. Do not say that the war against poverty failed because poverty cannot be defeated by money. Rather, say that the war against poverty failed because the people of America quit.

What Bishop Moore might have added were some of the splendid results of the Economic Opportunities Act of 1964: Head Start (which to this day we have never fully funded, even though we know how well it works), Job

Corps, Vista, Upward Bound, Foster Grandparents, Community Action. And let's not forget that these programs, which were launched in 1964, later helped produce Medicare and Medicaid and food stamps. Nor should critics of the War on Poverty forget that not every defense contract has yielded a perfect product at minimum cost, not every space launching has succeeded, and no cancer program has yet produced a cure.

Another pseudo fact that we need to dethrone is that the economic and social problems of the country are largely due today to giving minorities an even chance. This belief is spectacularly out of touch. The 800,000 farms lost in the 1980s weren't lost to blacks (who themselves lost thousands of farms); the thousands of manufacturing jobs lost didn't go to blacks. In fact, an estimated two million jobs in the '80s left the country in pursuit of low wages and high profits.

Scapegoating always arises when, instead of facing real wrongs, people are maddened with imaginary ones. It often appears that the more harm we white Americans do black Americans, the more harm we claim they have done us. We grab everything for ourselves, even the injuries!

But I part company with cynics who believe whites are so bankrupt that it is futile to appeal to their consciences. Many white Americans understand that, however complicated it may be to implement, there is a need for affirmative action. It is prompted by years of negative action. Without affirmative action, the first steps toward admitting blacks would never have been taken. "Equal opportunity" only reflects good intentions; affirmative action registers results.

It is also important to keep recalling, as does Jesse Jackson, that racial justice, and also gender equality, are morally and constitutionally "center." To call those promoting them "leftist" is dishonest, something usually done by right-wing politicians who appeal to the political center by attacking the moral center.

It is sad to hear even good Christians now say that we can't afford to resume the War on Poverty. If God is never spare when giving change, why should we hoard our pennies? If Christ died for us, can't we bleed just a little for him? The fact of the matter is, the country cannot afford *not* to resume the War on Poverty. Our cities lurch toward chaos and nihilism. Ghetto children have parents in their teens and twenties doing all the wrong things. Churches and schools have lost their moral authority. These kids are virtually alone, and the young black ones among them are caught in a vicious circle: joblessness leads to drugs, which lead to crime, which worsens the image of young black males, which makes it all the more difficult for them to find jobs.

A further reason why we have to resume the War on Poverty is because the quickest way to lose your humanity is to begin to tolerate the intolerable.

There is no substitute for a serious federal commitment. Historically, the national government has done the most for poor and exploited people—more than states and private enterprises. Americans know that the Declaration of Independence calls "self-evident" not only human equality but these truths as well, that all people are "endowed by their Creator with certain inalienable Rights, . . . Life, Liberty and the Pursuit of Happiness." What Americans forget is the next sentence, which states that governments are instituted among people "to secure these Rights."

The high and primary purpose of government is to *secure inalienable rights.* In the minds of our spiritual forebears, all else was secondary.

The Constitution also lays out a positive rule for governments. It mandates the President and Congress not only "to

provide for the common defence," but no less "to insure domestic tranquility," to "promote the general welfare, and secure the blessings of liberty to ourselves and our posterity."

When President Bush clamored for a reduction in the
capital gains tax, I knew such a step represented more
capital for capitalists, but not necessarily more jobs for the
jobless, let alone homes for the homeless.

By contrast, although hardly fond of military contracts, I
was impressed when President Carter's Secretary of the
Army, Clifford Alexander, in the course of four years, increased Army contracts with minority businesses from $98
million to $1 billion. And I'm intrigued by the idea of al-
lowing anyone who invests in the stock of an inner-city
enterprise zone to write off 100 percent of his or her investment up to $50,000 in the year the investment is made.
These two governmental measures represent not more
spending, but an investment in the future productivity of
minority citizens. By helping to vanquish their sense of im-
potence, they seek "to insure domestic tranquility," and
"promote the general welfare."

Most of all, we need policies fit for kids. As John Ben-
nett has written: "The surest test of the justice in a society
is the effect of its policies on its children." Currently one in
five of our children lives below the official poverty level,
and 100,000 are homeless. The Washington-based Children's Defense Fund urges three things: (1) *A healthy start,*
by providing the basic health care that so many families
cannot afford (29 percent of all American children have no
private health insurance); (2) *a head start*, by fully funding
Head Start programs, quality preschools, and child care;
and (3) *a fair start*, by ensuring families a minimum level
of economic security. This can be done through jobs, re-
fundable tax credits for families with children, and
stronger enforcement of child support laws.

Once again it must be pointed out that dollars spent now would save taxpayers more later in medical, education, prison, and welfare costs.

Obviously, government has to be held closely accountable for the money it spends. Also it can't do everything. Poor people must continue to play an important role in their own deliverance. Every pastor of a poor congregation knows how demeaning and paternalistic it is to treat the poor only as objects of forces beyond their control, as if they were not capable of acting on their own behalf. And to hold them responsible for a lot of what goes wrong in their families, their work, and their neighborhoods is not to blame victims so much as it is to empower them.

For middle-class people, a big job is to monitor their attitudes. For instance, Christians may not condone violence, but none has the right to condemn it without pointing out what produced it. Generally it is not extremists, but extreme conditions. Why ask, "Who lit the match?" instead of, "How come there was a fuse attached to a powder keg?"

Violence needs redefinition. It should mean anything that violates human dignity, human rights. Exploitation is the essence of violence, and its perpetrators can engage in it without ever drawing a knife or squeezing a trigger. Unfortunately, public attention is usually drawn to the situation only after the exploitation has produced a physically violent reaction, and then the public tends to be more repelled by the bloodshed than by the injustice producing it. Needless to say, the media help little, inclined as they are to sensationalize rather than to analyze. And by referring to rioters as vandals and hoodlums, politicians and the media take the burden off society for its failure to face the conditions that prompted the riots.

Malcolm X was always being attacked for advocating that African Americans should return nonviolence with nonviolence, and violence with self-defense. He put it more colorfully: "Be peaceful, be courteous, obey the law, respect everyone; but if someone puts his hand on you, send him to the cemetery."

To call turning the other cheek "masochism," as Malcolm did, was profoundly to misunderstand Christ, Gandhi, and King. But he was absolutely right to insist that civil rights be called human rights and that their violation in America should be brought before the United Nations. It galled him that a liberal Supreme Court justice in the 1960s, a presumed friend of blacks, could call the UN's attention to the plight of three million Jews in the Soviet Union and then not do the same for thirty million African Americans. If apartheid in South Africa could be condemned by the UN, why should racial discrimination in America be called a domestic issue?

White American students are often bothered by African Americans banding together in predominantly white universities. Their doing so reflects another of Malcolm's beliefs, that "before uniting with others it's well to unite among ourselves." If the result sometimes is black racism, it is to be deplored. Hatred (unless directed at stupidity or bigotry) is a diminishing emotion. It makes us inmates in prison houses of our own spirits. But black racism is not to be condemned without recognizing what produced it— white racism. And whites must remember that "reverse racism" is not the same as racism, for racism is properly defined as "prejudice plus power." Without power it seldom harms others. I think white Americans who are upset have to demand of themselves more of the patience and endurance they have long observed and admired in black Americans.

When signing the Economic Opportunities Act in 1964, President Johnson warned: "The war on poverty is not fought on any single, simple battlefield and it will not be won in a generation. There are too many enemies: lack of jobs, bad housing, poor schools, lack of skills, discrimination; each intensifies the other."

And there are other enemies. A nation that puts so much stress on getting ahead has a hard time dealing with those who fall behind. If you're successful, you seldom identify with failure. This is proved by the fact that integration of races has already resulted in an even greater segregation by class. The so-called "underclass" has all the marks of a subordinate caste. In the long run, I believe, class will prove a tougher nut to crack than race.

But let us not lose heart. Our contrition should diminish our pride, not our hope. Like few other enterprises, a war on poverty joins love and need. Remember, we are not called on to finish the task, only never to lay it aside. As the poet says, "We are only undefeated because we go on trying." And, of course, there's no reward like the sense of undeserved integrity that comes with being in the right fight.

6

SEXISM

"If the world were a logical place, men would ride sidesaddle."

Rita Mae Brown

"You [men] are not our protectors. . . . If you were, who would there be to protect us from?"

Mary Edwards Walker

"Can we imagine that, carrying out his mission today, the Christ of charity and unity would have restricted his circle to men alone?"

Anna Quindlen

NOT LONG AGO I heard a telling remark. Four of us went out to dinner. Two were women in their forties, intense, intelligent, and down-to-earth. In no time the other man and I found ourselves watching them "turn each other on" in the most amazing way. First they sniffed the air, delighted to find they were wearing the same perfume. Then their excitement increased when they discovered that each had driven up to the restaurant listening to a tape of the same singer. Then, with the same animation, they went on to discuss intractable political problems and deeply personal ones. Afterward, I said to one of them, "Except for the joy of watching and listening to the two of you, Don and I didn't have to be there at all."

"Oh, no," she replied. "You had to be there. We're very heterosexual, just homospiritual."

I understand—and envy not a little—the "homospirituality" of women these days. It must be wonderfully supportive and comforting. These two women were strong "feminists," defined as those who know that the only alternative to being a feminist is to be a masochist. They are aware that ever since the human race began, in almost every corner of the globe, misogyny—male fear and hatred of women—has been the order of the day. They also realize that the answer to misogyny is really androgyny, that is, the recognition that to some degree we are all both feminine and masculine. To put it differently, the man most deserving of respect is the man in every woman, and the woman most in need of liberation is the woman in every man.

In the book of Genesis there are two distinct creation stories. In the first chapter, God creates men and women together: "male and female he created them" (ch. 1:27). But religions and cultures, almost without exception, have reflected the bias of the second chapter, the story in which Adam is fashioned first, then Eve from Adam's rib, her sole end and purpose being to help Adam.

In a brilliant review of male chauvinism entitled "First Adam, then Eve," psychotherapist James Hillman points out how, from Aristotle to Freud, in findings clothed in the unimpeachable language of objectivity, male scientists time and again have proved the inferiority of women (see *The Myth of Analysis*). They did it quite simply. Lacking exact knowledge, they allowed fantasy to intervene, thereby making exact knowledge even harder to come by. These scientists didn't believe what they saw, they saw what they believed and then proved their beliefs with what they saw. And, needless to say, they never lacked for a male public eager to cheer their findings.

We brothers owe our sisters profound apologies. We've loved and married them, occasionally charmed them, but we haven't taken them as seriously as we take ourselves. And the condescension continues; they feel it, and we still don't get it. We might if we realized that the true test of sexism is less in the workplace than in the home. It is in families that the cruelest discrimination against women takes place. It is there that wives are physically abused and where neither domestic drudgery nor caring for children is justly shared.

Beyond offering apologies and mending our ways, we men have also much to learn from women. Vulnerability is a great virtue, as Paul realized when he said, "Whenever I am weak, then I am strong."[1] Without it there can be neither honesty nor intimacy. Without vulnerability we don't really meet one another, we just bump masks. It's a great mistake to keep putting your best foot forward when it's the other foot that needs the attention. As a rule, women understand this much better than men.

Speaking of the elections of '92, National Public Radio commentator Cokie Roberts underlined that economics was as big an issue for women as it was for men, but women tended to approach the issue differently. Typically a woman would think to herself: I'm worried that my mother needs to get her Social Security and her Medicare; I've got a job at the library that's about to be cut back; my kids' school lunch program is in danger; and my brother-in-law has been laid off and he's moved in, so my grocery bills are going up.

Says Cokie Roberts: "A woman's response to the economy is to want more government. Men want fewer taxes." Obviously women, like members of various minorities, look to government to help them get a leg up in a society that discriminates against them. As a rule, it's white men who want fewer taxes.

But what interests me at this point is the more concrete quality in women's caring. It's what makes women such natural pastors. And I think it fair to say that, as long as women clergy are "pastoral," their male parishioners today tend to accept and even deeply appreciate them.

But now comes the rub—male chauvinism raises its ugly head and is upheld, alas, by many women in the church. A woman pastor in Memphis told me after a mid-week service at which I preached: "If you were to give that sermon in my church next Sunday, my parishioners would call it

---

1. 2 Corinthians 12:10.

'challenging'. Were I to preach it, they would say nothing. But on Monday the phone calls would come: 'Are you feeling better? You seemed a little upset and anxious yesterday'. And by Tuesday I'd be receiving cookies and cakes to which my children have become so attached that they are always urging me to preach more 'challenging' sermons."

Just as someone coming in from outside is better able to tell those inside how stuffy a room has become, so women and minorities are better able to gauge the injustices of our society. Their comments may make the rest of us uncomfortable, but doesn't God always afflict the comfortable as well as comfort the afflicted?

Troubling some church people, as well as many others, is inclusive language. Let me try a comparison. The sixteenth-century Spanish painter El Greco elongated fingers, noses, and other human features; showing great imagination, he dared to distort physiological detail to get at the mystery of human personality. With similar imagination, biblical writers tried to portray the even greater mystery of God by deliberately distorting human relationships. To show the transcendence of God, they called God "King of kings and Lord of lords." To show that God cared for each of us as if God had naught else to care for, they called God "Father." It was a very imaginative use of language, for obviously God is only symbolically, not literally, either king, lord, or father.

But the language is culturally conditioned by patriarchal times, engendering patriarchal images. And to our more democratic way of thinking, the hierarchical imagery is somewhat oppressive. If inclusive language can still symbolize transcendence and caring and also be less offensive, then it's hard to object to new language simply because we're used to the old. Actually many of us, men and women, have become so accustomed to inclusive language that we find noninclusive language far more intrusive.

At Riverside Church in New York City I objected to singing new but clearly inferior hymns simply because their language was inclusive. Or if we sang better older hymns, I would object to our committee on inclusive language's altering verses at the expense of their poetry. When speaking to the committee chairperson, I said, "Your committee may have some major philosophers, but it also has some minor poets," his smiling response was, "Lots of idols, Bill."

Yes, the chairperson was a "he" and he was right to see that putting taste before truth and clinging to tradition for tradition's sake were forms of idolatry. I am reminded of T. S. Eliot's comment: "Those" he said, "who call the King James version of the Bible a monument to English prose generally mean a monument over the grave of Christianity."

Inclusive language is only the tip of the iceberg. If today's women's revolution succeeds, its theological influence will be comparable to the Protestant revolution of the sixteenth century. God's love, for example, will be exalted above God's power, and cooperation among God's children will seem far more important than competition. Church life will become increasingly warm, communal, egalitarian.

It is very hard to forgive someone who has hurt you deeply—even when you're well aware that what you can't possibly condone you can only forgive. So I am amazed that more women don't hate men. I suspect it's because they don't allow men to define them, that they know, as did Eleanor Roosevelt, that "It takes two for one to feel inferior."

Far too many women are today being battered and raped. Far too many have yet to receive equal pay for equal work, while millions await the states' ratification of the Equal Rights Amendment. To right such stubborn wrongs is clearly more pressing than to promote inclusive language. Nevertheless, I believe there is cause for tempered optimism when in America more and more women are being elected to political office, and when in Great Britain the Anglican Church votes to ordain women. It is only a matter of time before the Roman Catholic and Orthodox churches follow suit. *God* has not ordained patriarchy, not permanently, not ever, neither in the home, in society, nor in the churches. Those who, quoting scripture, think otherwise fail to realize that no word of God is God's last word.

"There is no longer male and female; for all of you are one in Christ Jesus."[2] We have had almost twenty centuries to implement Paul's revelatory moment. Christian men who still refuse to acknowledge their oneness and equality with women will continue not only to try to walk all over women at home, at work, and in the churches; climbing up on the cross to be seen from afar, they will also trample on the One who has hung there so long.

---

2. Galatians 3:28.

7

HOMOPHOBIA

Defense Department regulation, as of 1992:

> The presence in the military environment of persons who
> engage in homosexual conduct or who, by their state-
> ments, demonstrate a propensity to engage in homosexual
> conduct, seriously impairs the accomplishments of the mili-
> tary mission. The presence of such members adversely af-
> fects the ability of the Military Services to maintain
> discipline, good order and morale . . .

Defense Department regulation more than fifty years ago:

> . . . the necessity for the highest possible degree of unity
> and esprit-de-corps; the requirement of morale—all these de-
> mand that nothing be done which may adversely affect the
> situation . . . the enlistment of Negroes (other than for mess
> attendants) leads to disruptive and undermining conditions.

"Queers can't bond, the shrinks informed us. It's not you,
said the [Roman Catholics], it's the act we despise. And
you find somebody to love and prove them all wrong at
last, and still the fury boils inside you because the liars
made you grow up in a cage."

Paul Monette, Becoming a Man: Half a Life Story

TOO MANY CHRISTIANS use the Bible as a drunk does a lamppost—for support rather than for illumination. This includes even the scholarly ones, a conclusion I reach after reviewing much of the writing about scripture and homosexuality. While the research is impressive, the arguments on both sides strike me as either simplistic or too tortuous to be convincing. Why can't Christians just admit that there is such a thing as biblical deadwood, not to say biblical folly?

To pretend to be shocked at such a suggestion is pure hypocrisy, unless of course you still believe in slavery—"Slaves, obey your earthly masters" (Eph. 6:5); or in the inferior status of wives—"the husband is the head of his wife" (1 Cor. 11:3); and wouldn't dream of eating barbequed ribs, for to do so would be an abomination, *toevah*—the same Hebrew word used in Leviticus for homosexual acts.

The one piece of scholarship I did admire was a four-page pamphlet. On the cover side was the question, "What did Jesus say about homosexuality?" The two inside pages were blank, and on the back of the pamphlet was written, "That's right, nothing!"

It's time we grew up. It's time to realize that any belief in biblical inerrancy is itself unbiblical. Read the story of Peter and Cornelius (Acts, ch. 10) and you will see that scriptural writings do not support the inerrancy of scripture. Besides, Christians believe in the Word made flesh, not in the Word made words. Christianity is less a set of beliefs than it is a way of life, and a way of life that actually warns against absolute intellectual certainty: "O the depth of the riches both of the wisdom and knowledge of God! How unsearchable are God's judgments and God's ways past finding out! For who has known the mind of God?" (Rom. 11:33, KJV, alt.).

I think we know far more of God's heart than we do of the mind of God. It's God's heart that Christ on the cross lays bare for the whole world to see. And "God is love, and those who abide in love abide in God, and God abides in them" (1 John 4:16)—that passage suggests that revelation is in the relationship. And a relationship with God provides more psychological certitude than intellectual certainty. Faith is not believing without proof, it is trusting without reservation. I think all belief systems that rest on absolute intellectual certainty—be that certainty the doctrine of papal infallibility or the doctrine of the verbal inerrancy of scripture—all such belief systems should go out the stained-glass windows, for they have no proper place in church. They induce Christians to sharpen their minds by narrowing them. They make Christians doctrinaire, dogmatic, mindlessly militant. To such absolute belief systems can be attributed all manner of unchristian horrors such as inquisitions and holy wars, witch burning, morbid guilt, unthinking conformity, self-righteousness, anti-Semitism, misogyny, and homophobia.

Every Christmas I marvel at how the word of the Lord hits the world with the force of a hint. Naturally enough, we want God to be God, but God wants to be a human being, a babe in a manger. We want God to be strong so that we can be weak; but God wants to be weak so that we can be strong. Christ came to earth, not to overpower—

he came to empower. He came to provide maximum support but minimum protection, and it is precisely his support that should make Christians stop sheltering themselves between the covers of the Bible as house martins nest under the eaves.

Emily Dickinson wrote: "The unknown is the mind's greatest need and for it no one thinks to thank God." Well, I do. I thank God not only for all the wisdom in the sixty-six books of the Bible, but also that "the Lord hath yet more light and truth to break forth from his word." So I pray that the Lord will save all of us from three things: the cowardice that dares not face new truth, the laziness content with half-truth, and the arrogance that thinks it knows all truth.

Clearly it is not scripture that creates hostility to homosexuality, but rather hostility to homosexuals that prompts some Christians to recite a few sentences from Paul and retain passages from an otherwise discarded Old Testament law code. In abolishing slavery and in ordaining women we've gone beyond biblical literalism. It's time we did the same with gays and lesbians. The problem is not how to reconcile homosexuality with scriptural passages that condemn it, but rather how to reconcile the rejection and punishment of homosexuals with the love of Christ. It can't be done. So instead of harping on what's "natural," let's talk of what's "normal," what operates according to the norm. For Christians the norm is Christ's love. If people can show the tenderness and constancy in caring that honors Christ's love, what matters their sexual orientation? Shouldn't a relationship be judged by its inner worth rather than by its outer appearance? When has a monopoly on durable life-warming love been held by legally wed heterosexuals?

Beware of ministers who offer you the comfort of opinion without the discomfort of thought. The worst are the

TV "evangelists" (those children of a "looser" God!). Not content with calling homosexuality a sin, they go on to declare AIDS a form of divine retribution on homosexuals. If doctors don't know the cause of AIDS, you can be sure ministers don't either. And to suggest that a God of love would root for a virus that kills people, that a God of justice would wage germ warfare on sinners and not go after war makers, polluters, slum landlords, or drug dealers, all of whose sins affect others so much more profoundly—such a suggestion represents, in an apt phrase from Alcoholics Anonymous, "stinking thinking."

What AIDS does is raise heavy-duty questions for which many of us are not quite ready. One example: Along with straight children, gay children need to be taught that promiscuity is dangerous to their physical, psychic, and moral health. If, as most of us still think, example is the best form of teaching, then gay children have the same need as straight children to see loving, stable couples. If gay and lesbian couples show the same deep and abiding love for each other as do straight couples—and demonstrably they do; the evidence is all around—then why shouldn't the state offer the same civil marriage available to straight couples, with all the benefits that marriage entails, including the all-important-these-days death benefits?

Why shouldn't the Christian church do the same? Is John Fortunato, an Episcopal psychotherapist, wrong to formulate the issue as he does? "As evidence increasingly emerges that homosexuality is a natural biological variation in the human species, is it not time for the smug heterosexual majority to give up its self-image of monochromatic normality and acknowledge God's right to a pluralistic creation?"

Much ado is made about ordaining gay men and lesbian women. The fact is, many already are in the clergy and serving altogether as well as straight clergy. Most, of course, are "in the closet." What's so sad and ironic is that their congregations' love for them is based on a deception, and such an unhealthy and needless one.

The United Church of Canada has found a simple solution: it bases ordination on membership. If homosexuality doesn't exclude you from membership in a church, it can't exclude you from ordination.

When for ten years I was at Riverside Church, I watched the gay community of New York City, a community drenched in grief, reaching out to AIDS victims. The Gay Men's Health Crisis instituted hot lines, issued health packages, organized buddy systems so that no one would be alone, developed legal resources to protect their members against eviction and loss of medical insurance and care. And I watched gay members of our church be, one to another, shining examples of pastoral care. As they awaited death, as they all did, for themselves or their friends, the grace of God shone in their faces.

I think of them whenever the suggestion is made that we build more weapons at the cost of untold billions that could better be invested elsewhere—in the research, for example, necessary to find a cure for AIDS. And I think of them whenever I hear Christians say, "We must be patient; it will take time before the churches and the country accept homosexuality." Yes, let's be patient with bigotry at the expense its victims, those who are suffering the most and least deserve to be abandoned.

Homophobia, the fear and hatred of homosexuals, is bigotry. It is on a par with racism and sexism. In some ways it's worse: I've heard teenage gay and lesbian children tell of the pain that comes when the three main institutions of society turn their backs on them. They have in mind their families, their schools, and their churches. That kind of pain deserves to be met not with patience, but with holy impatience.

In a culture as prejudiced as ours is still, it is doubtful that many of us, gay or straight, will completely overcome our homophobia. What did most to help me battle mine, more than the accumulation and analysis of the evidence available, was to spend time with gay people. Familiarity bred only respect, never contempt.

"There is no fear in love, but perfect love casts out fear." (1 John 4:18) It is love that banishes fear and prejudice, that allows us to grow in understanding, freedom, and compassion. It was love that made Jesus draw to himself those whom the world abandoned. We who live in his name can do no less.

8

ABORTION

"O Divine Master, grant that I may seek
not so much to be understood
as to understand . . . "
from St. Francis' "Prayer for Peace"

Is THE UNBORN CHILD from the very first a child? Or is there a magic moment when prenatal biological life becomes human? Or does human life begin with the first breath? Obviously, on the answer to these questions hang all the law and the prophets of the morality of abortion.

Tennyson contended that "nothing worth proving can be proven, nor yet disproven." Nowhere is this contention more poignantly true than in the debate over abortion currently tearing this country apart. Called on to make a judgment, the Supreme Court did on January 22, 1973, in the now famous case of Roe v. Wade. Speaking for the majority of justices, Justice Blackmun held that "the term 'person' does not include the unborn." But he was talking constitutional law. The Court said explicitly that it was giving a legal, not a moral, definition of unborn life. The Court's decision proved once again how unsatisfactory legal definitions can be, if only because civil law has such a low tolerance for moral ambiguity. Actually, the Court implied something akin to a moral definition by dividing pregnancy into progressive trimesters, with different values assigned to each—from no value, to some value, to considerable value.

Nor are we helped by science which, like the law, cannot morally define when life begins nor, for that matter, when it ends. Science can tell us when a heart starts beating and when a brain is dead, but science cannot tell us when it is morally right to cease all artificial supports for a dying person, because science is not in a position to declare, "This is no longer a human being." It is the business of science to provide the *facts* of natural life, not the *values* of human life. In other words, when human life ends and when human life begins are not medical judgments but moral mysteries, and as such can be neither proven nor disproven.

The debate on abortion is hardly new. Christian opposition to it arose in large part out of opposition to infanticide, the barbaric custom of exposing to the elements and abandoning unwanted children, mostly baby girls. Writing in the third century A.D., Tertullian insisted that "*Homo est et qui est in futurus*" (a person who is ever going to be a person is one already). He argued "*etiam fructus omnis iam in semine est*" (because the fruit is already in the seed). But centuries later, when infanticide was practiced far less, Thomas Aquinas wrote that a fetus had to be "ensouled," or animated, before it could be considered a person. Thus from the Middle Ages to modern times abortion in the early weeks of pregnancy was generally not viewed as taking life.

Personally, my heart responds to Tertullian. A feeling of awe at the mystery of human life makes me want to believe that an unborn child is a child from the very start. Once fertilization is complete, the living entity is genetically human. It represents nascent life, deserving protection, and the defense of the defenseless has always seemed to me one of the crowning glories of Christian ethics.

On the other hand, my mind is compelled far more by Thomas Aquinas and what used to be the more traditional Catholic developmental view of life. It struck me as farfetched, to say the least, for the Missouri legislature a few years ago to pass a law that called a fertilized egg a human being "with all the rights, privileges, and immunities available to persons, citizens, and residents of this state." I remember wondering not only about the constitutionality of such legislation, but also whether teenagers in Missouri would now start applying nine months earlier for their driver's license, and their grandparents nine months earlier for their Social Security!

And what are we to say of the anguish of a woman— say, a mother, who lives in the slums of Rio or Chicago with more children than resources to keep them alive and well? She doesn't consider the new life in her womb as merely tissue or, as might a landlady, an undesirable tenant. No, it's her future baby. Only she's caught between two bad choices, both tragic. If she decides for an abortion, are we to say, as some do, that her motive has the "moral malice of murder?" Both heart and mind are repelled by such a total divorce of motive from action. And mind and heart both have to respond to women who ask how it is that so many who rejoice at humanity's awesome power to change nature refuse to grant women control over their own procreative power. And why should women be punished for abortion and not men for failing to use contraception? Furthermore, today's world, as we all know, is hardly unpeopled. As I've earlier suggested, family planning everywhere is imperative. Soon all inhabitants of the globe may be called on to decide who will live and who will die, and who will decide. In such a radically new situation, could it be that we are falsely sanctifying the whole reproductive process?

What is certainly clear is only the irony of those who preach the sanctity of even unwanted pregnancies and then attack nutrition programs for pregnant women, Aid to Families with Dependent Children, and food stamps. And if women still are paid only 74 percent of what men make and 100,000 American children are homeless, then all of us ought to be paying a lot more attention to the sanctity of life of women and children already born.

There is a real problem in calling a crime something a great many people don't even consider a sin. To criminalize abortion would not of itself instill a sense of the sanctity of prenatal life. Only education can do that. So a state-enforced anti-abortion policy could never have the pro-life consequences that the pro-life movement claims. Such a policy would reduce only the number of legal abortions, not significantly the total number of abortions. While to many pro-lifers such an action might be emotionally satisfying, it could hardly be considered morally so. And that is why so many thoughtful religious people are, in effect, anti-abortion and pro-choice. They feel, as did the Supreme Court members in 1973, that the government simply has no role beyond protecting a woman's right in the first trimester to make her own choice.

One of the criteria for a good law is its enforceability. An anti-abortion law would surely prove as unenforceable as the Prohibition laws of the 1920s, which were finally repealed in 1933. A national anti-abortion law would also create a small army of quack practitioners. It would cruelly penalize legitimate physicians trying, according to their own lights, to be humane as well as law-abiding. It would create extortionists "shaking down" both legitimate and illegitimate practitioners. Most of all, it would bring great suffering to innumerable women, mostly poor women.

Many wish more unmarried women would consider, rather than having an abortion, bearing their children and giving them up for adoption. But that's asking a lot when a moral stigma attaches itself to both the mother and her baby in many an illegitimate birth. The ancient Romans changed the legal definition of an illegitimate child from *filius nullius* to *filius populi*—a child "of the people," a child belonging to everyone. It would certainly reduce the number of abortions if in all our minds we made the same conceptual change, and also expanded maternity leave and child-care opportunities.

Because human beings cannot agree on a moral definition of unborn life, abortion will remain a moral dilemma. And the worst thing we can do with a dilemma is to resolve it prematurely because we haven't the courage to live with uncertainty. People will remain divided, focusing either on the fetus as an object of value or on the woman as a moral agent who must have freedom of choice.

Fortunately contraception poses much less of a problem. If we would improve methods of contraception, and through religious and secular education raise our standards of moral responsibility, the day might come when abortion would no longer be the heart-wrenching social issue it is today, for the simple reason that it would rarely any longer be necessary. Meanwhile, whether it is taking or preventing life—whichever our belief—abortion remains at best a mournful undertaking.

9

CAREER VERSUS CALLING

"To each is given the manifestation of the Spirit for the common good."

St. Paul, 1 Corinthians 12:7

"One often passes from love to ambition, but one rarely returns from ambition to love."

La Rochefoucauld

"My object in living is to unite
My avocation and my vocation
As my two eyes make one in sight.
Only where love and need are one,
And work is play for mortal stakes,
Is the deed ever really done
For Heaven and the future's sakes."

Robert Frost, "Two Tramps in Mudtime"

I HAVE A PERSISTENT FANTASY about what happens to the idealism of college students. It goes like this: College-bound youth arrive on campus with ideals. Their parents want them to have ideals; so do their teachers; so do they. But they also have ambition, else they wouldn't be going to college. Being smart, it doesn't take them long to figure out that what American society promotes as belief and what American society rewards as belief are markedly different. So there arises in students' minds a painful question: What am I going to park—my ideals or my ambition? The usual answer, reached rapidly and surely, is, It would be a shame to abandon my ambition. Only now it is called "self-fulfillment," "self-actualization," or some other term from the juiceless jargon of the sociological trade.

But what to do with the ideals? No student wants to put them out with the garbage. So students find a closet where, well-wrapped, they carefully store their ideals. Then, returning to "self-realization" they decide to go on to graduate work—say, to law school. They do well, and upon graduation join the prestigious firm of Airdale, Airdale, Whippet, and Pug. Their astronomical starting salary is exceedingly "self-fulfilling." Shortly thereafter they meet the girl/boy of their dreams, get married, move to the suburbs, and have children. And then they remember—the ideals. So they go to the closet, unwrap the ideals, turn to their children, and say, "Here, kids, play with these."

And that, my fantasy told me, is how in America today some of us keep our ideals alive. I'm glad to say it led me to more serious thoughts about the difference between a career and a calling. Without doubt the two can be, and often are, combined. But they can also be distinguished. A career seeks to be successful, a calling to be valuable. A career tries to make money, a calling tries to make a difference.

Professor William May of Southern Methodist University has pointed out that the words "car" and "career" come from *carrera,* the Latin word for racetrack. This suggests that a car and a career both have you going in circles rapidly and competitively. There are also other similarities. A car is an auto-mobile, a self-driven vehicle. It frees you from traveling with others. To Professor May it represents "glass-enwrapped privacy as you speed down public thoroughfares toward your own private destination."

"Calling," on the other hand, comes from the Latin *vocatio* (vocation), from *vocare,* (to call) which was defined by a seventeenth-century Puritan divine as "that whereunto God hath appointed us to serve the common good."

A career, we can say, demands technical intelligence to learn a skill, to find out how to get from here to there. A calling demands critical intelligence to question whether "there" is worth going toward. If something is not worth doing, it's not worth doing well.

People interested in a career read best-selling books such as *Swimming with the Sharks, Winning Through Intimidation, Looking Out for Number One.* A calling, by contrast, seeks the common good, not private gain. It sees service as the purpose of life, not something you might consider doing in your spare time. It is not against ambition, but considers ambition a good servant and a bad master.

You might say that a career helps you win the rat race; a calling reminds you that even if you win a rat race, you're still a rat!

College career-placement offices rarely reflect the tension between a career and a calling. But I once saw a sign on the door of one such office that read: "To hell with your career; what's your calling?" And some college students once showed moral imagination by circulating a pledge that read: "I pledge to seek only such employment as will benefit my fellow human beings and not harm the environment." The expectation was not that everyone would sign, only that everyone's consciousness would be raised.

Rarely do university faculty and administrators recognize the degree to which every country's education reflects that country's ideology. For example, in Cuba it is believed that as no person is self-made, every person owes some self-expenditure for the common good. If, for example, you graduate from the medical school in Havana, you are dispatched to some distant impoverished barrio and gradually work your way back to the fleshpots (and there are only a few) in Havana. And because every country's education reflects that country's ideology, universities in Cuba, and Cubans generally, have a serious civil-liberties problem.

In our country civil liberties fare better, although we always have to enter the usual caveats such as A. J. Liebling's "A free press is a great thing if you can afford to own one." But because a country's education reflects that country's ideology, in our case the freedom properly enjoyed by faculty and students to think and say pretty much what they will—that freedom is vastly exalted over any obligation to do any good to anyone.

When the clarion call of society is "Enrich thyself," it is naive to think that the humanities automatically humanize. Likely as not they are but a cultural icing on an economic cake, particularly if they are taught by professors who can lead emotionally satisfying lives without finding moral excitement in the subjects they teach.

In contrast to a few years ago, when power was based more on gender, race, and whom you knew, power today is generally based on knowledge, and on knowledge generally acquired at a university. This means that universities are now graduating their students into the so-called "ruling class" without questioning how they are going to exercise their power. As we all know, millions of college graduates earn incomes in cities in order to pursue private happiness in suburbs, leaving the inhabitants of cities in sub-Saharan conditions.

Should such a narrow career orientation concern chaplains only and not college presidents, deans, and faculty? Is it too much to ask a university to recognize that the acquisition of knowledge is secondary to its use, that basically universities have but one moral issue to face, and that is: "Now that we have all this knowledge, what *in the world* are we going to do with it?"

It's worth asking whatever happened to that earlier understanding of the higher calling, the call to serve the common good? Hannah Arendt claimed that it was unfortunate for Americans when the phrase "life, liberty, and the pursuit of happiness" gradually came to mean exclusively "private happiness." Two hundred years ago John Adams talked frequently of "public happiness." He objected to taxation without representation, not because the taxes were large (they were minuscule), but because the representation was nil. To deny people the right to participate in decisions that affect their lives was to John Adams to deprive them of public happiness.

As we have altered the meaning of happiness, so we have altered the meaning of freedom. To our Revolutionary forebears, it was practically synonymous with virtue, as it was to Abraham Lincoln when he called for a "new birth of freedom." Freedom to Lincoln was not the freedom to do as you please; it was the freedom to be pleased to do as you ought.

Returning to Revolutionary times, Sam Adams said: "We may look to armies for our defense, but virtue is our best security. It is not possible that any state should long remain free where virtue is not supremely honored."

Said John Adams: "Our Constitution was made only for a moral and religious people. It is wholly inadequate to the government of any other."

All our early American leaders had read Montesquieu, who differentiated despotism from monarchy from democracy. In each of these forms of society he found a governing principle: for despotism it was fear, for monarchy it was honor, and for democracy it was virtue. Because freedom was practically synonymous with virtue, we turned out a generation of politicians named Washington, Jefferson, Adams, Franklin, Hamilton.

Today with a population eighty times the three million who were Americans in 1776, we don't produce leaders like that anymore, and the reason is clear; as Plato said, "What's honored in a country will be cultivated there." We have wonderful athletes and generally inferior politicians, and we deserve them both. Because we have so cruelly separated freedom from virtue, because we define freedom in a morally inferior way, we have entered what Herman Melville called the "Dark Ages of Democracy," a time when, as he predicted, the New Jerusalem would turn into Babylon, and Americans would experience what he called "the arrest of hope's advance."

Small wonder, then, that careers are winning hands down over callings. In the absence of a good society, it's hard to be a good person. In a bad society, common integrity is made to look like courage. As a Le Carré character observes, "You have to think like a hero to behave like a decent human being."

But decent human beings are still everywhere to be found, people who see life as service, as a calling to serve the common good. I know a doctor who returned from the Peace Corps and opened an inner-city clinic in Cleveland. It multiplied, and twenty-five years later the Norwood clinics serve 58,000 low-income patients.

I know another doctor who, in Memphis, not only opened a church-related clinic but persuaded nearly a hundred other doctors in Memphis to take care of a certain number of poor patients free of charge.

And I know a third doctor, the leading peace activist of Salem, Oregon. When I asked him how he happened to become an eye doctor, he replied, "It stems from my commitment to peace. People rarely have emergencies with their eyes. So appointments can be scheduled during the day, which leaves evenings free for my peace work."

Several law schools are now allowing their students to choose a calling over a career. If, upon graduation, they work three to five years for legal-aid societies or other public-interest groups and make no more than $25,000 a year, the law schools will forgive the loans they accumulated during their years of study. Why shouldn't medical and business schools do the same?

There is much to be said these days for a program of national compulsory service for all Americans. I have in mind a service, say, of two years between the ages of seventeen and twenty-two. Beyond the Peace Corps, participants could choose to join a health corps, a conservation corps,

an urban development corps, a business corps—different
services doing work that is currently neglected in areas important and useful to the nation. Or people could serve
their two years in the private sector in organizations such as
Jobs for Peace or Peace Action for a Sane World. National
service activities wouldn't be only for the educated, but
would be designed as well to advance the skills and knowledge of undereducated participants, making literacy in English one of several overall goals.

I believe the 1990s may well begin in '93. By that I
mean the generous and intelligent self, long dormant in so
many Americans, will awake and begin to assert itself. The
year 2000 should be a great goad. Who wants the new
century to witness the continued shedding of the tears and
blood of the innocent? Already I sense a new willingness
to tithe time as well as money to serve the common good.
All of us, at any age, with or without college degrees, can
work for peace, for social justice, and for the preservation
of the environment. All of us, at any place, can speak out
against bigotry in all its nefarious forms. No one is useless
in this world who lightens the burden of it for anyone
else. And no one makes a greater mistake than those who
do nothing because they can only do a little.

"This little light of mine, I'm going to let it shine." Those
who have attended a candlelight service or been on a candlelight march know how much more inspiring are thousands of little flames than those giant lights that illuminate
ballparks. All of us who have read Jesus' parables know
that when God gives the talents—even one—we must give
the effort. Besides, serving the common good is so much
more fulfilling, less boring, than pursuing private gain. If
it's sometimes more painful, that's all right: in pain we are
more alive than in complacency.

I believe that God is calling each and every one of us to
show up, to "double the heart's might," to help one another

build a more just and generous society at home and a genuine, viable global community that hates war and holds nature in reverence. Our calling today is like God's call to Moses: arising from the world's pain, it is a call to alleviate that pain by sharing it. And with so much in bud, the moment is so ripe.

EPILOGUE

A WORD TO THE PREACHERS

"If it's both true and painful, say if softly."

Advice from Larry Dunham,
Yale freshman

DEAR COLLEAGUES,

Perhaps this will surprise some of you, but like most of you I much prefer pastoral counseling to prophetic preaching. It surely is one of life's highest privileges to be invited into the inner recesses of another's spirit, to listen to a troubled soul honestly struggling to come to terms with his or her life.

But pastoral counseling and prophetic preaching cannot be neatly separated. Already I've indicated how devastating to warm hearts was the Cold War. And when homophobia is a thorn in the flesh of the church, how can pastors remain silent? The answer is simple: We can't. The only question is how best to deal with matters that are controversial.

Whenever possible, I believe we should challenge people kindly. Nothing, for example, prevents any of us, in the middle of a sermon, from saying, "What I now want to say is hard for me to say, so I can imagine how painful it's going to be for some of you to hear. But here we are in church, where unity is based not on agreement, but on mutual concern. So let me tell you what's on my mind and heart and, after the service, those of you who disagree can bring your coffee into the library and tell me where you think I went wrong."

Obviously we should always be able to state the opposition's position to the opposition's satisfaction. It's helpful to speak confessionally. As regards homosexuality, for instance, there are basically only four positions a person can take: punitive rejection, nonpunitive rejection, conditional acceptance, and unconditional acceptance. While Pat Robertson and Jerry Falwell represent the first position, most of your parishioners, I would guess, are nearer the third. To lead them to the fourth, first tell them how you used to find yourself where they are now, and then how you came to see that position as untenable.

Why is it that we are so loath to talk about controversial issues? I can think of two basic reasons. The first is that we wouldn't feel confident about what to say. Unlike rabbis, who on an average read three times as much as do ministers or priests, we tend to be grossly underinformed, and to the degree that our ignorance stems from our complacency it is an ethical, not an intellectual default. Why don't we consult our former seminary professors? Why do we so hesitate to call local teachers and college professors? And what about our own parishioners? It's my experience that they are generally delighted to steer us toward good reference material. When I was chaplain at Yale, I rang the phones off the hook of the Divinity School faculty. I did the same later with the professors at Union Theological Seminary. For the ten years I was at Riverside Church, every Sunday morning at eight o'clock I picked up the phone to read my sermon to Richard B. Sewell, a retired English professor who had once taught Yale students creative writing. (Fortunately, he was wise enough to know there were only so many changes one could make before eleven o'clock!)

If we're white, we should make a point of listening regularly to African Americans. If we're men, we should do the same with women. Straight people should have more discourse *with* than *about* homosexuals. And we all need close Jewish and Muslim friends.

Good preachers are lifelong learners. I believe we should tell our parishioners that, while we want to be apprised immediately of any emergency, in the absence of emergencies we're going to consider mornings up to eleven o'clock a time for study, prayer, and preparation. When our preaching and teaching improve, they'll be grateful.

A second reason for avoiding controversial issues is the deep need of so many pastors to be loved. This, I believe, is a serious matter. All of us have benefited from true friends, whom I consider to be those willing to risk their friendships for the sake of their friends. Quite different are those pastors fearful of saying anything that would imperil the love of their parishioners.

Let's try an exercise. Suppose you've said a few controversial things in the course of a Sunday sermon, and after the service, at the door, an irate parishioner warns you: "Say anything like that again, and that's the last time you'll see me in this church." What is your immediate reaction?

Is it (with a nice smile), "I guess I did my duty today." Or are you more apt to say, grasping his hand with both of yours, something like, "Oh, I'm so sorry you feel that way. Let me come by for a cup of coffee. I'm sure we can work it out. I'll call you to set a time."

While I'm all for approaching controversy in the most pastoral way possible, I think we need to remember that Jesus never withheld the telling word if only the telling word would serve. Recall as well Saint Augustine's contention that there are as many wolves within the fold as there are sheep without. Though the estimate is perhaps exaggerated, his thought is hardly surprising. If the essence of evil is disguise—pretending something bad is really something good—and if the best disguise in the world is the cloak of religious piety, where else, if not in church, would you expect to find evil people? As Pascal said, "People never do evil so cheerfully as when they do it from religious conviction." My point is this: don't good shepherds have a certain duty to drive out the wolves to make room for more sheep?

I raise the question because I think it's a complex one pastors almost invariably avoid. Ideally, we should stay engaged both to our parishioners and to the issues that so vitally affect the lives of all of us.

"Caring is the greatest thing, caring matters most." So, in his dying breath, said the great British layperson Baron von Hügel. If we who are preachers want our people to lend us their ears, we must first give them our hearts. And if we do, then because of our love for them we shall never be afraid to put at risk their love for us.

It's my own deep feeling that most people in the pews are far more prepared for painful truths than we give them credit for. What they want their preachers to do is to raise to a conscious level the knowledge inherent in their experience. And the majority of them realize that the painful truths known and spoken sour and subvert life less than those known and unspoken. So let us not hesitate to speak up, to preach with clarity and compassion a true and lively biblical word, remembering always that our calling is to serve the Lord, not to be servile to our congregations.

As I write, the morning papers carry the news of the death of Supreme Court Justice Thurgood Marshall. It was he who, in a fourth of July address, said:

> We must dissent from the indifference. We must dissent from the apathy. We must dissent from the fear, the hatred, and the mistrust. . . . We must dissent because America can do better, because America has no choice but to do better.

Thurgood Marshall was a hopeful man. He understood that hope criticizes what is, hopelessness rationalizes it. Hope resists, hopelessness adapts.

So, dear colleagues,

Lots of hope,

William S. Coffin